PRAISE FOR STEVEN'S INS

I so look forward to your week... know of any other spiritual author that I enjoy more; nor has any other spiritual author written more ideas that have created "ah-ha" or "light bulb" moments in my thinking. I deeply appreciate your ministry. You are a blessing to all who receive your messages or read your book.

~ Lynn Jacobson, Surprise, AZ

Every time I re-read your messages, Steven, I immediately find myself right back "in the flow!" Your reminders are so clear and accurate! Thank you so much!

~ Vickie Dulaney, Oklahoma City, OK

Steven, I want you to know that your weekly messages are some of the very few that I get a restorative message from. Yours always seem to hit the nail on the head. Bless you for sharing your learning process with me. It fits my life so well.

~ Lori Peterson, Amarillo, TX

I can't thank you enough, Steven, for your inspirational messages. You have no idea how much better they always make me feel, especially when I am dealing with difficult situations. Again, many, many thanks!

~ Sandra Winter, San Antonio, TX

Steven, thank you for your amazing, inspiring, and incredibly wise messages every Sunday, and for your continued commitment to bringing these teachings into the world.

~ Cybie Mauro, Syracuse, NY

I can't tell you how much your Sunday messages mean to me, Steven. I don't currently have a church home, and I often feel lost on Sunday mornings. But then I turn on my computer, and there you are, ready to fill my need! I just wanted you to know how thankful I am for you and your work.

~ Hilda Pillers, Manassas, VA

I really look forward to your weekly messages, Steven. They are always calming, encouraging, and uplifting. I clearly feel that you are God's instrument to help guide us and soothe us.

~ Rebecca Johnson, Dallas, TX

Steven, I always keep each weekly message handy so I can read it again every day. I have read many books and heard many speakers talk about being in the divine flow, but your approach is by far the most direct and comprehensible.

~ Susan Sutherland, Monterey, CA

I get more out of your weekly messages, Steven, than I do from a combination of all the other messages that I receive. I believe that we all have life teachers that speak particularly to us. You have become one of those teachers for me. And I know that many others feel the same way. Bless you!

~ Sheri Huffman, Garland, TX

Steven, you are the most insightful expert on the nature of the divine flow that I have ever encountered. Your weekly messages are gentle, loving, intelligent, witty, and straight to the point. Every Sunday I look forward to reading your consistently illuminating perceptions.

~ Linda Anderson, Sedona, AZ

Thank you for your ministry, Steven, on behalf of the many people, including me, whom you may never meet face-to-face. We are out here, and we very much appreciate you. You have made a positive difference in many lives—in mine, for sure.

~ Jean Jaeger Pfeifer, Madison, WI

Steven, your messages always seem to arrive just when they will do the most good for me! Thank you for sharing yourself in this way, and for making this your life's work. You really are making a difference in the universe.

~ Megan Doren, Dallas, TX

FURTHER DOWN
THE STREAM

FURTHER DOWN THE STREAM

101 More Tips for Living Life in the Divine Flow

STEVEN LANE TAYLOR

Enlightenment
Lane
SEDONA, ARIZONA

FURTHER DOWN THE STREAM
© 2012 by Steven Lane Taylor
Cover photograph by Cosmo Condina
Author's photograph by Marla McDonald

For more information, please contact:
Enlightenment Lane, the Publishing Division of
Steven Lane Taylor, LLC
1020 Crown Ridge Road
Sedona, Arizona 86351
info@rowrowrow.com

ISBN-13: 978-0615611129
ISBN-10: 0615611125

To Carol ~
For blessing me with your
unending love and support.
I am eternally grateful.

Contents

Introduction

No doubt about it, life can be a struggle. Achieving your goals and realizing your dreams can be incredibly difficult. But how much of that struggle is unnecessary? How much of that difficulty is actually avoidable? Much more than you might think. Whether you are consciously aware of it or not, there is an underlying current in your life—a divine flow—that is continually guiding you toward the *effortless* fulfillment of your heart's desires. The challenge is learning how to *recognize* and *cooperate* with that flow, instead of inadvertently blocking your experience of it.

ABOUT
ROW, ROW, ROW YOUR BOAT

In my first book, *Row, Row, Row Your Boat: A Guide for Living Life in the Divine Flow*, I used the lyrics to a well-known children's song as a simple set of instructions for experiencing the divine flow in your life more freely and more frequently. Again, those instructions are:

Row, Row, Row Your Boat,
Gently Down The Stream,
Merrily, Merrily, Merrily, Merrily,
Life Is But A Dream.

When examined word by word, this lyrical metaphor reveals a powerful and effective formula for living a life of greater happiness, satisfaction, and ease.

The word "stream," for example, reminds you that to reach your chosen destinations in life, you never have to get there under your own power alone. There is always a current beneath you—a divine flow—that is *helping* you get there. It is a flow that opens doors for you and provides opportunities for you. But most of all, it *guides* you—constantly telling you the next right step to take. It guides you through your own intuition, through the intuitive wisdom of others, and through divine signs and synchronicities.

To "row" is to *act* on that divine guidance, and to refrain from taking actions based solely on your own limited intellect. In order to row *with* the flow—rather than *against* it—you have to let go of what you think you know, and never force things to go the way *you* think they should go. In other words, you must be willing to row "gently"—continually adjusting to the course of the current, even when it is heading in a direction that you don't understand.

That kind of flexibility requires a "merry" mind-set on your part, because nothing interferes with your ability to cooperate with the divine flow more than negativity. To be open and receptive to divine guidance, you must maintain a positive state of mind, and look at every "bend in the stream" as just another stepping-stone to your highest good.

Those are just a few of the ideas explored in *Row, Row, Row Your Boat*. Much more is revealed, of course, including the importance of maintaining present moment awareness, the necessity of releasing your attachments to specific outcomes, and the essential role that love and forgiveness play.

ABOUT
FURTHER DOWN THE STREAM

Shortly after the publication of *Row, Row, Row Your Boat*, I began writing weekly inspirational messages that expand on the principles I shared in that book. *Further Down The Stream* is a compilation of 101 of those messages, offering readers an enhanced understanding of the divine flow through additional details, stories, insights, and examples.

If you have been receiving my messages via email, or you have been reading them on Facebook or my blog, you will notice a number of differences. Many of my messages have been updated to reflect the passage of time. Other messages have been revised or refined to include what I have learned about the divine flow in recent months. Some messages have been combined into a single message. Others have been grouped together to form a logical series.

Scattered throughout this book, you will find messages that focus on special occasions such as Easter, Mother's Day, Thanksgiving, and so on. To mimic the way those occasions arise during the calendar year, I have placed these messages at very specific points within the book. For the most part, though, the messages included in *Further Down The Stream* are in no particular order . . . which allows you three different ways to read this book and receive value from it:

1. You can read this book as you would read any book—straight through, from the first page to the last.

2. You can open this book randomly and read whatever message your eyes fall upon. This enables your inner sense to guide you to a message that might be especially helpful to you at that particular point in time.

3. You can search through the Table of Contents for a specific subject. For instance, if things aren't happening fast enough for you, "When The Flow Seems Slow" will help you understand why. If you are curious about meditation and how it enhances your ability to be in the flow, my four-part series on "The Value of Meditation" will answer your questions. If you are facing a difficult challenge in life, you will find several messages offering insights in that area, including "Purposely Choosing Challenges" and "Turning Problems into Possibilities."

Naturally, this book will serve you much better if you have already read *Row, Row, Row Your Boat*. But even if you haven't, the concepts presented in *Further Down The Stream* are easily understandable. And to help make sure of that, the first four messages in this book have been purposely placed there to lay a foundation for many of the messages that follow.

No matter how you decide to read *Further Down The Stream*—whether you choose to read it from front to back, or you decide to skip around—I trust that you will find the messages in this book to be helpful, uplifting, informative, and inspiring. Here's to living life in the divine flow . . . and here's to discovering how joyful, fulfilling, and remarkably effortless the journey of life can be.

I

Do You Know
What You Want?

At the beginning of a new year, it is common for people to spend some time visualizing what they want to manifest for themselves in the coming twelve months—what they want to have, do, or be by the end of the year. Do you do that? Or, are you a person who *doesn't* spend any time picturing what you want, because you don't *know* what you want?

"I don't know what I want" is something that I hear fairly often in my workshops and retreats. And to be perfectly honest with you, it's an issue that I don't relate to very well. Personally, I have never had any trouble identifying what it is I want to have, do, or be in my life. I just abide by the old adage, "follow your bliss." I notice what makes me the happiest, and I focus most of my time, attention, and energy on manifesting more of that.

If you are a person who claims to not have any specific goals or dreams in life—if you feel like you don't really know what you want—I invite you to consider this: Perhaps you *do* know what you want. Perhaps you *do* know what you would like to have, do, or be. And perhaps you *do* know what makes you happy. Maybe you just aren't willing to admit it to yourself. So you nip the idea in the bud before it ever fully develops.

And why would you do that? There are various reasons why. Among them are these: You don't consider yourself worthy enough to have, do, or be what you want. You don't think you are smart enough to achieve it, or capable enough to handle it. Or, your goal is so lofty, your dream is so ideal, you can't conceive of how such a manifestation could ever be possible. So you literally stop the thought before it ever fully forms in your mind.

Dear reader, if any of this resonates with you, then please know this: *If you can dream it, then you deserve to have it!* Remember that as a holy and wholly loved Child of The Divine, you are *innately worthy* of whatever it is you want to have, do, or be in this life. Don't worry about how you're going to manifest it. That's not your job. That's the job of the Universe! In fact, the Universe wants nothing more than to help you fulfill your *every* heart's desire . . . *just because you desire it!*

Don't edit yourself. Go ahead and dream big! Begin picturing your ideal life today. Heck, begin picturing it right this very minute! And let your imagination soar!

2

The Divine Origin
of Desires

In my last message—the one titled, "Do You Know What You Want?"—I said that the Universe wants nothing more than to help you fulfill your every heart's desire . . . just because you desire it! Well, believe it or not, there are many people in this world who think that the key to happiness lies in *suppressing* or *eliminating* their desires. Desire itself is perceived to be—ironically—an *undesirable* aspect of our human nature. And that perception is understandable, because problems can definitely arise from having desires. For instance:

- If you are overly attached to having a desire manifest in one particular way, that can be a problem.

- If you believe that you can't be happy until a certain desire is fulfilled, that can be a problem.

- If the desire to accumulate possessions becomes an obsession, that can be a problem.

Notice, though, that in those examples, the desires *themselves* are not really the problem. The problem is how those desires are being *handled*. It is, indeed, very important for you to carefully monitor how you are *managing* your desires. But that doesn't mean that you have to *deny* yourself the pleasure of having desires and pursuing their fulfillment. In fact, I believe that trying to do so will only result in greater unhappiness.

Why? Because you are an individual expression of that infinitely creative energy that is frequently called—appropriately enough—*The Creator*. That means that you, yourself, are a Divine Creator at heart. What you call a "desire," is something that is born—in its *purest* form—at the very core of your being, where your Creative Spirit resides. Your desires are simply *intentions of your Spirit* to create something in this world that didn't exist before . . . including experiences.

In other words, having desires is not so much an aspect of your *human nature,* as it is an inherent, inescapable, and glorious part of your *spiritual nature*. If you are suppressing your desires, you are not allowing your Creative Spirit to express itself, and happiness becomes impossible.

So again, as I see it, having desires is not really a problem. If there is a problem, it is keeping your desires in their *proper perspective*. And what is that proper perspective?

Remember that for everything you "think" you want in your *mind*, there is a deeper, underlying desire of your *Spirit* that initiated that idea. It is that *pure desire of your heart—unaltered* by the intellect and *uncorrupted* by the ego—to which the divine flow is guiding you. And that means you must be willing to follow the flow to something that may be quite *different* from what you are expecting.

Remember, too, that in the end, the happiness you feel from actually *fulfilling* your desires is just the icing on the cake. Never forget that true, long-lasting happiness doesn't come from reaching your chosen destinations in life. *True* happiness comes from enjoying the journey there . . . and from expressing love to everyone you encounter along the way.

With those two perspectives in mind, dear reader, go ahead and desire away! As I encouraged you to do in my last message, feel free to imagine whatever it is you want to have, do, or be in life . . . and go for it! After all, that's just the Creator within you creating!

3

Desires of the Heart

As I mentioned in the preceding message titled, "The Divine Origin of Desires," no matter what it is you "think" you want in your *mind*, there is a deeper, underlying desire of your *Spirit* that initiated that idea. It is that *pure desire of the heart*—a desire *unaltered* by the intellect and *uncorrupted* by the ego—to which the divine flow is guiding you. And that means you must be willing to follow the flow to a destination that may not be anything like what you planned on or expected.

So how—*exactly*—is a desire of the *heart* different from a desire of the *head*? Briefly stated, your heart—which is synonymous with your Spirit—is much more interested in manifesting an *experience of life* than it is in acquiring *material possessions*. And that experience of life will usually have the following qualities:

- It will fulfill you in a truly deep, lasting, and meaningful way.

- It will always be in the best interests of all involved—not just you.

- It is likely to be an experience that is greater and grander than what you originally desired.

For example, you may "think" you want a particular house that is up for sale. You may even believe that the Universe is directly supporting you in the fulfillment of that desire, because you get a "good feeling" every time you drive by that house. But the fact is, that house might represent a certain experience that your Spirit wants to have—an experience of comfort, abundance, or even love of family. And it is *that experience* to which you are being divinely guided, which may or may not have anything to do with that specific house, or any house at all!

Keep in mind that if you cling too rigidly to what you specifically "think" you want, you are likely to wind up frustrated or unfulfilled. You either *won't* get where you want to go, because the Universe really isn't supporting you in arriving at that particular destination . . . or—through your forceful efforts—you *will* get there, only to discover that your desired destination is, in the end, unsatisfying or fraught with problems.

That doesn't mean that you have to refrain from visualizing what it is you "think" you want, or that you have to stop giving your desire any attention. There's nothing wrong with focusing on a particular dream, and holding on to the essence of that dream. The key is to avoid becoming overly attached to each and every *detail* of how you see that dream materializing, or what it has to *specifically* look like. Your role is to be willing to cooperate with the unfolding of a *higher* good, knowing that the divine flow is always guiding you to either what you want . . . to its equivalent . . . or to something even better.

One way to eliminate or minimize this whole issue right from the start is to make sure that your goals and dreams are as close as possible to what your heart wants. And how do you do that? Become heart-centered. Each day, spend some time in prayer and meditation to get in touch with the truth of who you really are at the core of your being . . . which is Divine Love itself.

When you shift your sense of identity away from what you *look like* and what you *do,* and identify instead with the *Divinely Loving Spirit* that is your *true essence,* you will discover that the desires that arise in your mind are much more faithful to how they were first conceived by your heart. And, like all desires of the heart, they won't be limited or self-serving in nature. Instead, they will be divinely inspired ideas that are grand and glorious and good for all.

So, if you want to be in the flow from the very *start,* then the first thing you should do is get into your *heart!* Focus on being the love that you are *at heart*—on being the compassionate, kind, caring, and forgiving person that you are at the center of your being. Do that, dear reader, and the desires of your heart will *become* the desires of your head!

4

Identifying Intuition

When reduced to its simplest essence, living life in the divine flow is about one main thing: recognizing and following divine guidance. Although you can receive divine guidance through signs and synchronicities, and through the wisdom of other people, the most valuable, reliable, and consistent guidance that you receive is through your own intuition—from the Divine Spirit within you that is speaking to you. Intuitive guidance can take many forms, such as:

- A thought that suddenly pops into your head

- A still, small voice that you seem to "hear" from within

- An image or a vision that appears in your mind

- A particularly vivid dream that you have

- A physical sensation that gets your attention

- A simple feeling of peace or "rightness"

- A "Knowing"—that is, an inexplicable and
  unshifting sense of surety

To be and stay in the flow, it is important to recognize how your Spirit usually communicates with you, to nurture that sense, and to begin to rely upon it heavily.

The big question is this one: How do you distinguish intuitive guidance from other thoughts or sensations? How do you know if that still, small voice you are hearing is the voice of your Divine Spirit, or the voice of your self-serving ego?

As you may have guessed, there is no hard and fast rule for decisively determining whether a thought or a feeling is of divine origin. However, if you are in doubt, it does help to ask yourself this one simple question: "Does the guidance I am sensing *fit the nature of my Spirit?*" To help you answer that question, here are four different aspects of your Spirit's nature, with a description of how those aspects affect the type of guidance that you receive:

1. Your Spirit is one with all.

In Spirit, there is no place where you end and someone else begins. In Spirit, we are all part of One Universal Whole. That means that you will never receive intuitive guidance that obviously harms or diminishes another person, because that person—in Spirit—is just another part of "you." Intuitive guidance will always be in the best interests of *everyone*.

2. Your Spirit is all-knowing.

Being intimately connected to the Omniscient Mind of the Divine, your Spirit is aware of an almost *infinite* number of ways for you to move forward in life successfully. That means that you will never receive intuitive guidance that seems to *demand* that you do one thing in particular because that's your "only option." Your Spirit will simply *suggest* the course of action that happens to be the most beneficial one for you to take at that particular moment in time. And if that course of action is never taken, or it eventually ceases to be the most beneficial direction for you, your Spirit will then simply make a *new* suggestion. In other words, intuitive guidance may—for a time—be *persistent*, but it will never be *insistent*.

If you have a strong feeling to take immediate action on some kind of opportunity, and you are feeling anxious because you think that kind of opportunity may never come again, be careful. That insistent feeling is probably *not* your Spirit speaking to you. It is likely to be coming from your ego—that fear-based part of you that believes in lack and limitation, and can cause you to act impulsively.

3. Your Spirit is always positive.

The energy of your Spirit is a positive energy. That means that your Spirit will generally express itself in a positive way, suggesting a positive action-step for you to take. Rather than saying, "Don't do this," intuitive guidance is much more likely to say, "Do this."

4. Your Spirit is indestructible and eternal.

Your Spirit cannot be injured, or cease to exist. That means that your Spirit knows nothing of fear. It knows only the peace that comes from being one with All-That-Is, and the joy that comes from the human experience—of just being alive and in the world. Generally then, intuitive guidance will feel peaceful or joyful. If you are in immediate physical danger, yes, you may receive intuitive guidance that feels extremely powerful. And you might react apprehensively to such a strong suggestion. But the guidance itself will not be infused with fear, because it will not be coming from a place of fear.

I know two people whose lives were saved by a very clear and direct inner voice. One message was simply "Get off the road now," which prevented that person from colliding with another vehicle. The other message was "Quit what you are doing and leave the river," which saved that person from drowning in a flash flood. In both instances the voice of Spirit was very powerful. But even so, behind that voice there was still an underlying sense of eternal well-being. Because well-being is all that Spirit knows.

Like I said, there is no single, definitive way to identify intuitive guidance. But if that guidance is peaceful, positive, persistent, and in the best interests of all, that's a good indication that you are receiving divine direction. May those four qualities enhance your ability to tell when your Spirit is speaking to you. And may you be willing to make the decision, or take the step, that your Spirit is suggesting.

5

Trusting Intuition
Over Intellect

Have you ever had an intuitive feeling that was completely at odds with what your intellect was telling you? Have you ever had an inner knowing that contradicted all logic and reason? Dear reader, when *common sense* tells you one thing, but your *intuitive sense* tells you another, *follow the guidance of your intuition!* Like I stated in my preceding message titled, "Identifying Intuition," your intuition is the most valuable, reliable, and consistent source of divine direction that you have. And when you honor that inner sense of direction—no matter how subtle it is—you will be amazed by how easy it can be to fulfill your heart's desires.

I'll never forget the time when Carol and I accomplished three different goals of ours in a very unexpected manner. We lived in Dallas, Texas at the time, and we thought that it would take at least one week and three separate trips across town to accomplish all three missions. Carol wanted to go to a special store to find some fabric to re-cover an ottoman; I wanted to go to a particular bookstore to see if they would stock my recently published first book; Plus, I wanted to get in contact with a man who had offered me a very lucrative writing project. This gentlemen had promised to give me all the details I needed in order to do the work, but he had suddenly stopped answering the phone and replying to emails.

One day, when Carol and I were out running a few errands, Carol noticed that we happened to be passing by the fabric store that she wanted to go to. Even though we were on a toll road that had limited exits, I agreed with Carol that it would be logical to stop at the store while we were in the area. But as I approached the exit, something just didn't feel "right." I questioned that intuitive feeling, because stopping right then would obviously make the most sense. But the closer I got to the exit, the less "right" it felt.

Suddenly, the thought popped into my mind that it would be better to come back later. Come back later? What an inefficient use of our time that would be! Dallas was a big city, and coming all the way back to this part of town couldn't possibly be the right thing to do. Surprisingly, though, when I considered that option, it *did* feel right—*very* right!

So, even though it was more efficient to stop at the fabric store while we were right there, I followed the advice of my inner guidance. We passed the exit, continued down the road, and finished up our errands.

Now, here's where the story gets good. Since the fabric store was on a toll road, I had to figure out the best way to get back to it. And the best way just happened to go right by the bookstore I wanted to visit. Sensing that this was "the flow," we stopped at the bookstore. We discovered that the store wasn't open on that particular day of the week.

Coincidentally, though, the manager was in the store that day, anyway. She noticed Carol and me through the window, and for some reason came over and opened the door for us. When I introduced myself, the manager said she had already heard of my book, and would like to purchase some copies right then and there—if I had any with me. I did!

That mission accomplished, Carol and I then continued on to the fabric store. As Carol looked through the rolls of fabric, I suddenly heard a voice behind me say, "Steve, what are you doing here?" It was the wife of the man I had wanted to connect with! Her name was Michelle, and she was very surprised to run into me on her side of town—and in a fabric store of all places. But she was very happy to see me, because she had a message for me. As it turned out, Michelle's husband had been in Canada for several weeks. While there, he had lost his cell phone, and his laptop computer had crashed. When he was finally able to get in touch with Michelle, he asked her to find me and give me the information I needed so I could proceed with the writing project . . . which she did right there in the fabric store.

Remarkable! Instead of it requiring three separate trips over a period of a week, Carol and I fulfilled all three of our desires in one single hour, with absolutely no planning or foresight on our part. By following my inner guidance, Carol and I wound up in exactly the right place, at exactly the right time . . . time after time.

The lesson here is simple. Your intuition is continually directing you toward whatever it is you want to have, do, or be in life—continually! But to take advantage of that guidance you must be aware of the subtle ways that you are being directed, and you must be careful not to hastily dismiss or overrule that guidance because "you know better" or "it doesn't make sense."

If you want to be "in the flow," you must avoid forcing things to go the way you "think" they should go, and you must be willing to move in a direction that is different from what you expect . . . or what even seems reasonable! In other words, you must trust your *intuitive sense,* even when it seems to make *little sense!*

6

The Middle Way

One of my favorite movies—and especially Carol's—is "Little Buddha." Although two stories are depicted concurrently in this film, the basic tale is about Prince Siddhartha of India, and how he became the Buddha.

In a pivotal scene, Siddhartha witnesses a man teaching a boy to play a stringed instrument. The man tells the boy, "If the strings are too loose, they won't play. If they are too tight, they will break." It is at this moment in the movie that Siddhartha discovers the wisdom of "The Middle Way," an enlightened way of life that avoids extremes in favor of moderation.

This is not unlike the wisdom of "rowing with the flow." If you have no goals or dreams in life, you are too "loose." You are just aimlessly drifting. And living life in the divine flow is not about drifting. It's about actively participating in the manifestation of what brings you joy. It's about consciously choosing a destination and rowing towards it.

If you *do* have a destination in mind—a desire that you would like to fulfill—but you are pursuing that goal *relentlessly,* always pushing, driving, and forcing your way forward, then you are too "tight." And one day you may break.

Rowing with the flow is the middle way. You choose your destination, and you row towards it, but you row *gently*—pausing between each and every stroke of your oars to discern the next right step that you feel you are being *divinely guided* to take. You don't force things to go the way you think they should go, or try to control and manipulate specific outcomes. Instead, you remain flexible enough to continually adjust to the course of the current—willing to move in a direction that is different from what you expected, and even willing to arrive at a destination that is different from the one you originally set out for.

So, dear reader, what will it be? Do you want to drift through life listening only to the "music" created by the well-tuned instruments of *other* people? Or, do you want to create some "music" of your *own*? If it's the latter, just make sure that your strings are not too loose, *or* too tight. Remember to follow the middle way—attuning yourself to the divine flow. Do that, and whatever you manifest in your life will be especially harmonious.

7

Misconceptions About Manifesting

One of my favorite quotes is this one by the renowned Transcendentalist author, Ralph Waldo Emerson:

"The moment you make a decision,
the whole Universe conspires to make it happen."

If that is true—and, for the most part, I believe it is—then you can see what tremendous power you have when it comes to manifesting whatever it is you want to have, do, or be in life. You have the *whole Universe* working on your behalf to help you realize your dreams!

In a few popular books and videos, our helpful Universe is portrayed as a "genie" that magically delivers to you whatever it is you specifically ask for . . . as long as you stay focused on what you want. But is that true? Is the Universe like a giant genie?

My experience of life suggests that we do, indeed, have celestial assistance when it comes to accomplishing our goals and fulfilling our desires. But to me, the portrayal of the

Universe as a genie is overly simplistic. And I believe it leaves people with quite a few misconceptions about how the manifestation process really works.

In this message, I would like to briefly address four of those misconceptions.

MISCONCEPTION #1:
You must be very *specific* about what you want,
because you only get *exactly* what you ask for.

There is nothing wrong with being specific about what you want to get out of life. In fact, I recommend it. But after that, it is best to let go of any rigid attachment you might have to one specific outcome. My experience has shown me that the Universe is willing to help me manifest something that is even *better* than what I think I want—something that is greater, grander, and more fulfilling . . . and something that is always in the best interests of all. When I confine myself to my own limited, preconceived ideas about what I think is best for me, I risk missing a much greater miracle.

MISCONCEPTION #2
You *literally* attract what you want *to* you.

Is it possible to ask the Universe for something and have it literally show up on your doorstep the very next morning? Yes, actually, it is. I have done that very thing. But that kind of experience is rare. What you *are* always attracting to you are the people and circumstances that *lead* you to what you want. Through synchronistic events and happy coincidences, the Universe will open doors for you and create opportunities for you in direct response to your desire. But you have to go through those doors and take advantage of those opportunities! In short, you have to act! If you are just sitting around waiting for something to *literally* fall in your lap, you may be waiting quite a while . . . perhaps forever.

MISCONCEPTION #3:
It takes a lot of concentrated thought and energy
to manifest what you want.

Really? Time and time again I have manifested something in my life without giving it a second thought—often within 24 hours! The key is not telling the Universe what you want over and over again. *The Universe hears you the first time!* The key is being totally open to *receiving* what you want, and *paying attention* to what immediately appears in your life—no matter what that might look like. It's okay to spend some time visualizing what you want, and getting in touch with what brings you joy. Just remember to keep *most* of your focus in the here and now, because that's where your miracle is going to manifest.

MISCONCEPTION #4
You must be *consciously* aware
of what you want, and ask for it.

On more than one occasion, the Universe has demonstrated

to me that it knows exactly what I need, even when I am not consciously aware of it myself! When I cooperate with the Universe by doing what I feel divinely guided to do at any given moment, I consistently end up manifesting things I greatly need, but never thought to ask for. If you want to have a similar experience, then listen to your intuition; heed the divine signs and synchronicities that are all around you; and move in the direction that seems indicated—even if you have no idea where you are being guided.

So, dear reader, I ask the question again: Is our Universe like a genie that can only respond to our stated desires in a very automatic, robotic-like fashion? Based on my experience, I say no. This wonderfully beneficent Universe is far more intelligent than many people are giving it credit for these days.

Whether we call it "The Universe," "Source," "Divine Mind," or "God," experience after experience suggests to me that there is, indeed, a *Higher Intelligence* that is at work in this world. It knows what is in our *hearts*, as well as what is in our *heads*. It knows what we *need*, as well as want we *want*. And it is *already* working on our behalf to fulfill our dreams, goals, and desires . . . whether we have specifically asked for something or not.

Let's not get so caught up in our power to manifest, that we forget to be grateful for the *Higher Power* that is behind it all . . . a Power that always has our best interests in mind, and is continually orchestrating the highest good for each and every one of us.

8

Something Better

In two of my previous messages, I said that the divine flow is not necessarily guiding you to what you specifically want. Instead, it might be guiding you to the equivalent of what you want, or to something that is even *better*—to something that is greater, grander, and more deeply fulfilling. That means if you want to manifest that better blessing, you have to trust the flow and follow its lead . . . even if you don't understand where you are headed!

The first house that Carol and I rented here in Sedona is a good example of "rowing with the flow," and manifesting something that was greater and grander than anything we ever imagined possible. Here's the story:

After attending a spiritual conference in Phoenix, Arizona in July of 2006, Carol and I drove up to Sedona to check out homes for rent. It had long been our dream to move to Sedona, and we wanted to see what was available to rent in this peaceful paradise, before we had to fly back to Dallas, Texas—where we lived at the time.

We had a list of a dozen homes to look at. The first

home on our list was a home that—from the description in the classified ad—seemed perfect. The price was right, the location was good, and Carol thought that she had made a special connection with the homeowner when they spoke on the phone. We couldn't wait to see it.

The last home on our list was last for a reason. It was on a golf course. Not being golfers, we just couldn't imagine how that house could possibly be the one for us, and we were in no hurry to see it. In fact, the only reason that this house was on our list at all was because it literally "came to us" via someone we happened to meet in Phoenix.

I'm sure you have already guessed where this part of the story is going. As it turned out, the home at the top of our list was not at all suitable. It was a place we wouldn't want to spend a day in, let alone years. Disappointed, but not discouraged, we then proceeded to look at the rest of the homes. There were a couple that would "do," but none that we really felt good about.

Finally, with every other home on our list crossed off, we reluctantly went to look at the house on the golf course. Wow! Were we ever surprised! We loved almost every single thing about this house. It had a huge covered patio, a really nice office, an oversized bathtub, a two-car garage, and lots of lush, green flowering bushes. And best of all, this particular home wouldn't be ready to rent until November— the exact month that Carol and I wanted to move! All the other homes required us to start paying rent immediately.

We felt like the divine flow had guided us to the perfect home, and we were glad that we had included it on our list, even though we had been reluctant about it. The only thing this house lacked was a view of Sedona's Red Rock formations, which is what Sedona is famous for. Although a Red Rock view would have given us a more "authentic experience" of living in Sedona, Carol and I weren't expecting to have that kind of vista, anyway. So we agreed to rent the house on the golf course starting in November, and we flew back to Dallas.

Now, here's where this tale takes an interesting turn. Believing that everything was all set with that particular property, Carol and I began to make plans for moving. We had already gotten pretty far "down the stream" when we received some distressing news from the woman in Arizona who had directed us to that house. To make a long story shorter, suffice it to say that this property was suddenly no longer available to rent.

Yikes! What were we going to do now? Should we fly back to Sedona to find another place to rent—any place— even if it meant we had to start paying rent right then and there? That's not what our inner guidance said. Our inner guidance simply told us to ask the woman in Arizona if she would be willing to keep looking around for something similar.

So we followed our guidance and asked her. The woman replied that she didn't really have time to do that kind of thing for us. Plus, she said it would be very unlikely for her to come across another house that was as nice as that one— especially one that would available at the time we wanted it. However, she said she would keep her ears and eyes open.

Although that didn't sound very promising, Carol and I

immediately noticed that we both felt an inexplicable sense of peace about the whole thing. In fact, we not only felt that we would still manifest a really nice house in Sedona, we had a feeling that it might be an even better house!

One week passed. Then two. It was getting close to the point where Carol and I would have to make some decisions about moving that couldn't be reversed. And yet, we still felt this inner sense of calm. And then the call came.

Through a series of synchronistic encounters, our "angel" in Arizona had heard about another home that would be available to rent right when we wanted it—in November. But this wasn't just any home. It was a home that was right down the street from the one we had originally agreed to rent. And we wouldn't even have to fly out to see it, because in its construction, features, and landscaping, it was almost identical to the other home! There was only one major difference between the two. This home happened to feature a direct view of Bell Rock, Castle Rock, and Courthouse Butte—three of Sedona's most popular Red Rock formations!

So, did the divine flow guide us to "something better?" I'll say! But I hope you noticed two very important things about this story—two things that contributed to its remarkable ending. First, although Carol and I couldn't imagine ourselves living on a golf course, we let go of our resistance just enough to go ahead and include that kind of house on our list of homes to look at. And second, when the house we wanted became unavailable, we did not hastily take matters into our own hands—that is, we did not immediately fly back to Sedona and rent something else out of sheer desperation.

Instead, we trusted that inner sense that told us that everything was going to be okay. We put our faith in the flow, and the flow came through for us beautifully.

Dear reader, I've said it before, and I'll say it again: We live in an incredibly miraculous Universe—a Universe that is continually working on our behalf to fulfill our every heart's desire, or its equivalent, or something even *better*. May we have the faith and patience it takes to cooperate with that divine flow of goodness in our lives. May we always be open and receptive to *all* possibilities. And may we consistently take the steps that we are being divinely guided to take . . . even if we're not sure where those steps are leading!

9

There's No Place Like Home

In my last message—the one titled, "Something Better"—I shared a story about the first house that Carol and I rented here in Sedona, and how the divine flow miraculously guided us to that wonderful home. Stories about peoples' homes—and the astonishing ways those homes have come into their lives—are among the most profound manifestation stories that I hear. But why is that? What makes manifesting a home so special? Is it somehow different from manifesting anything else?

In a way, yes, it is. As I frequently mention, most of the things you think you want in your mind, are really just symbols for what your heart desires. And it is the underlying desires of your heart to which the divine flow is guiding you. And what does your heart desire? Mostly, to have various experiences of life. And that's what makes a home so special. Because the right home can satisfy a *multitude* of experiences that you deeply desire to have.

For instance, in a world where we are constantly on the go, you may desire a sense of permanence, and the right

34

home can certainly offer you that—giving you a feeling that there is one place on this planet you can always come back to.

You may desire to express yourself creatively, and the right home can offer you endless opportunities for creative self-expression—from decorating to landscaping. It may even provide you with the perfect environment for other creative pursuits, such as writing, or painting, or building your own home-based business.

One desire that we all share is to express the love that we are at the core of our being, and there is usually no better place to love—and to be loved—than right at home with your own family.

Perhaps, too, you are seeking a little more comfort in your life, and a warm, cozy home can definitely provide you with that experience—both physically and emotionally.

So, when you are focused on a desire for a new place to call home, is it any surprise that the divine flow becomes more evident? Is it any surprise that coincidences happen more frequently, and miracles occur more freely? No, it is no surprise at all. Because everything that the Universe is doing to help you fulfill your desires for experiences such as permanence, creative self-expression, love, comfort, and more, may be *converging* on that *one, single manifestation!*

When it comes to manifesting the desires of your heart, there truly is no place like home. Perhaps the old song, *"Home, Sweet Home,"* says it best:

> *'Mid pleasures and palaces*
> *Though we may roam,*

Be it ever so humble,
There's no place like home.

A charm from the skies
Seems to hallow us there,
Which, seek thro' the world,
Is ne'er met with elsewhere.

Home, home, sweet, sweet home!
There's no place like home,
There's no place like home.

IO

Gratitude and The Flow

As you may know, Sedona, Arizona is considered by many to be one of the prettiest places on the planet. Shortly after Carol and I moved here, one of our dearest friends wrote to us and asked, "Do you pinch yourselves every day to make sure that you are not just *dreaming* that you live in Sedona?" Our answer was "Yes." We *do* pinch ourselves every day. But it's *not* to assure ourselves that we are not just dreaming. It's the opposite of that. We pinch ourselves every day to *remind ourselves* to be *grateful* for where we are living, and not take it for granted.

I am constantly amazed by how easy it is to take almost *anything* for granted—even this heavenly haven called Sedona. It takes very little for me to become distracted by the day-to-day details of living and working, and completely forget to appreciate the beauty that is all around me: the magnificent Red Rock formations; the brilliant orange sunsets; the profusion of purple blooms; and the abundance of wildlife right in my own backyard.

I bring this up, because one of the keys to living life in

the divine flow is to have an *attitude of gratitude*. And why is gratitude so important? Because when you are grateful, you feel good. And when you feel good, you are more open and receptive to divine guidance, and thus able to experience the flow's miracles more freely and more frequently.

The challenge is *maintaining* that attitude of gratitude for all of those things that you usually take for granted, such as your health, your home, and your helpful relationships. To live life in the divine flow it is important to be continually grateful for *all* of the blessings you have in your life—not just the *extraordinary* ones, such as receiving unexpected income, or miraculously avoiding an accident.

Take a moment right now to look around you. What are you taking for granted? And what, instead, should you be consciously grateful for? Pinch yourself, and begin to consciously count your blessings. You may be surprised by how quickly the divine flow gives you *even more* to be grateful for!

II

The Constant Possibility
of Good

In Shakespeare's *Hamlet,* you will find this wise statement: "There is nothing either good or bad, but thinking makes it so." Said another way, nothing *in and of itself* is inherently good or bad. *We* are the ones who assign meaning to things and label them as good, bad, or indifferent.

Well, if that's true—and I do believe it is—then what kind of attitude should we take about the different kind of circumstances that we experience in life? In some circles, the answer to that question is illustrated by the following fable:

There was once a wise old farmer who owned a prize horse. One day his horse ran away. Upon hearing the news, his neighbors came over to offer their condolences. "Such bad luck," they said sympathetically. "Maybe," was all the farmer replied. A few days later the horse returned, bringing with it three other wild horses. "How wonderful," the neighbors exclaimed. "Maybe," replied the old man again. The following day, the farmer's son tried to ride one of the untamed horses, was thrown off, and broke his leg. Once again, the neighbors offered their sympathy, saying, "How awful." "Maybe," answered the farmer one more time. The day after that, military officials came to the village to draft young men into the army, where casualties were running high. Seeing that the son of the farmer had a broken leg, they passed him by. The neighbors once again congratulated the farmer on how well things had turned out. "What good fortune," they said. The farmer replied yet again, "Maybe."

I appreciate this story for one particular reason. It illustrates the fact that we rarely, if ever, know enough to be able to accurately judge any circumstance as either good or bad. However, I wonder if there isn't a more positive way to respond to what we encounter in life.

I realize that the farmer's response was objective and non-resistant. And that kind of mind-set certainly elicits a feeling of peace, which is wonderful. But to me, the farmer's "maybe so, maybe not" attitude is somewhat flat and lifeless—limiting the possibility of feeling anything *beyond* peace, such as joy. And I, for one, believe that our Spirits are in this world—and in these bodies—to experience happiness and joy, as well as peace.

If something happens that I think is good (even though I know it is just a subjective judgment on my part), I want to be able to experience all the good feelings that come along with that. And when things don't seem to be going very well, I *still* want to experience good feelings! So how do I do that?

Like I have stated in previous messages, I simply look at every situation that "appears" to be bad, and see it as a stepping-stone to my highest good. And that's not just wishful thinking on my part. Similar to the circumstances described in the fable, it has been my experience time and time again that the possibility for good exists within every situation . . . and the divine flow is continually working on my behalf—and everyone's behalf—to manifest that good.

If you want a more positive and uplifting way to respond to life's circumstances—a way that promotes feelings of happiness and joy, gratitude and thanksgiving—then I invite you to approach life differently than the farmer did in the version of the fable that you just read. I invite you to consider the example set by the farmer in my own *alternative* version of this story:

> There was once a wise old farmer who owned a prize horse. One day his horse ran away. Upon hearing the news, his neighbors came over to offer their condolences. "Such bad luck," they said sympathetically. "I believe there can be good in this," the farmer replied. A few days later the horse returned, bringing with it three other wild horses. "How wonderful," the neighbors exclaimed. "Yes, it is good," replied the old man. The following day, the farmer's son tried to ride one of the untamed horses, was thrown off, and broke his leg. Once

again, the neighbors offered their sympathy, saying, "How awful." And once again, the farmer answered, "I believe there can be good in this." The day after that, military officials came to the village to draft young men into the army, where casualties were running high. Seeing that the son of the farmer had a broken leg, they passed him by. The neighbors once again congratulated the farmer on how well things had turned out. "What good fortune," they said. And one more time the farmer replied, "Yes, it is good . . . very good indeed!"

So, dear reader, the choice is yours. You can achieve peace by assigning little or no meaning to what occurs in life. Or, you can open yourself up to something more by seeing everything as good, or good in potential.

I, for one, choose to thoroughly enjoy all the "good" things that happen in life. And more than that, I choose to appreciate *the constant possibility of good* in everything else.

12

Whose Boat
Are You Rowing?

W hen it comes to living life in the divine flow, it pays to
remember that you rarely get anywhere in life completely
on your own. Reaching your chosen destinations in life usually
requires the assistance and cooperation of others. You need
their help to get down the stream, and they need *your* help.

Do you ever get the feeling, though, that you are
spending way too much time rowing someone else's boat?
Does it seem like you are always abandoning your *own* boat
in order to help someone else navigate life's waters? Like
everything else in life, there is a balance that must be reached
when it comes to offering help, as well as accepting help.

I remember a gentleman who told me about a day when
he was really "in the flow." He told me how every single step
that needed to be taken, was taken *for him* by various "Earth
Angels." He said that he really didn't have to do *anything* to
accomplish his goals for the day. All of his desires were fulfilled effortlessly!

As I delved deeper into this man's story, however, I
discovered that his "Earth Angels" were simply friends and

family members who were taking on responsibilities that—as far as I could tell—were actually *his* to take. He simply wasn't rowing his own boat, so others stepped in and rowed it for him. They were taking up the *slack* caused by his *lack* of action.

Dear reader, there will be plenty of times in life when another person *genuinely* needs your help. In fact, you may be in his or her life specifically for that very reason. But if you feel burdened by a request for help—if you feel obligated or resentful—that "heavy" sensation may be an indication that your assistance would actually be doing that person a disservice. Sometimes, the best help you can give others is to simply *show* them how to help themselves, and leave it up to *them* to take that action . . . or not.

Remember that when you are being *divinely guided* to help another person, there should be a feeling of "rightness" about it—a feeling of peace and ease. Those are the kind of feelings you usually experience whenever helping another person is your next right step—your *divinely directed* step.

That's not to say, however, that your divinely directed step is going to feel peaceful and easy in *every single instance*. Taking care of a critically ill or disabled loved one, for instance, can often feel burdensome, and even bring up feelings of anger and resentment. But if your assistance is *truly* called for—*divinely* called for—there will still be an *underlying sense* that helping this person is "the right thing to do."

Whether you are being *asked* for help, or you think you need a little help *yourself*, the key is to always take time to get quiet, go within, and get in touch with the wisdom of your Spirit. That's the only way you can accurately discern what is *truly* yours to do . . . or not do.

May we all row our boats *responsibly*—that is, may we take full *responsibility* for rowing our *own* boats, while maintaining the *ability to respond* to another's cry for help when it is genuinely needed.

13

The Beauty of Blind Love

February 14th is Valentine's Day, the day we make a conscious effort to express our love and appreciation to the people in our lives whom we dearly cherish. For the most part, the kind of love being celebrated on this special day is "romantic" love. And one of the characteristics of "romantic" love—at least in the beginning—is that this kind of love is "blind." We literally don't see the physical flaws and personality quirks in the beloved. He or she looks perfect to us.

But is that really being blind? Or is that seeing as we are truly *meant* to see—as that Universal Presence we call God, sees? As we grow in our spiritual understanding, aren't we called to see *beyond* appearances? Aren't we called to see *beneath* the physical, and look *past* the behavior? Aren't we called to see the true beauty and the radiant innocence of the Spirit that lies *within* each person? Aren't we called to see his or her *inner* perfection?

If that's being blind, fine! Give me some dark glasses and a cane! Because there is nothing that feels as good as truly loving. There is nothing that feels as good as recognizing the inherent goodness of another's soul, and allowing yourself to bask in that glorious light.

So what does this have to do with living life in the divine flow? Simply this: When you love as God loves, and see as God sees, it won't make any difference where you are along the course of "the stream." It won't make any difference whether you are just about to reach your dream, or whether you are still miles away from it. When you love without limits you are happy right where you are, wherever you are. And, in the end—all goals and dreams aside—isn't happiness all you really want out of life? Isn't happiness all you've been trying to get out of life . . . all along?

Well then, here's to "blind" love! And here's to having a lovingly happy day, *every* day!

14

The Value of Meditation
Part 1

One of the most common questions I am asked about living life in the divine flow is this one: "What can I do to improve my ability to be in the flow?" Notice the word, "do," in that question. These people aren't necessarily seeking a better understanding of the flow. Rather, they are looking for some kind of specific tool or technique that they can employ to experience the flow's miracles more freely and more frequently.

Well, as it turns out, there is something that you can "do" that will dramatically magnify the experience of the divine flow in your life, and I highly recommend it. That, quite simply, is to meditate, and to meditate on a daily basis.

There is nothing really mystical or magical about meditation. Meditation is simply a way of slowing down your thoughts. Generally, it involves focusing your attention on one solitary thing, such as your breathing, a comforting phrase, or a peaceful image. As other thoughts arise—as they invariably will—you *observe* those thoughts, but you don't let yourself get caught up in them. Instead, you simply allow those thoughts to pass by—like watching clouds floating across the sky—and you gently return your attention to the focus of your meditation.

And how, exactly, does that enhance your ability to be in the flow? Being in the flow is about recognizing and cooperating with divine guidance. And meditation dramatically increases your ability to be in direct contact with the guidance of your own inner Spirit.

Your Spirit is the most valuable and reliable source of divine guidance you have. You can always trust your Spirit to know what your next right step should be. And, through what is commonly called your intuition, your Spirit is always attempting to "tell" you what that step is. The trouble is, it is difficult to "hear" that still, small voice of your Spirit when your mind is full of noisy self-talk—that endless chatter in your head about what just happened, what it might mean, and what might happen next. A daily practice of meditation is an effective way to *quiet your mind,* and open up enough *gaps* between your incessant thoughts so the guidance of your Spirit can get through.

That guidance may not come to you during the meditation itself. But a regular practice of meditation— especially in the morning—can help you maintain a state of mind that is much more open and receptive to divine nudges throughout the day. Instead of automatically connecting one thought to another, and to another, and to another, you are more readily able to leave a little room *between* your thoughts. And it is through those *open spaces* that Spirit speaks to you. It is through the *gaps between your thoughts* that divine ideas can make their way into the world, often popping into your mind suddenly and unexpectedly.

In short, a daily practice of meditation helps you become more "open minded," so you are better able to intuitively sense divine direction, and clearly identify your next right step . . . that one *divinely guided* step that will keep you moving down the stream toward your dream with effortless ease . . . that one *divinely inspired* step that will help you be—and stay—in the flow.

Note: If you are new to meditation, and you would like detailed instructions about how to meditate, here is a webpage that describes the simple technique that I use: *www.alternative-medicine.net/meditation.*

15

The Value of Meditation
Part 2

In Part 1 of my series on The Value of Meditation, I said that a daily practice of meditation helps you live life in the divine flow by enhancing your ability to intuitively sense divine direction, and recognize your next right step. But that's not the only value of meditation. There is another benefit that I would like to share with you: A daily practice of meditation helps you *respond* to situations rather than *react* to them. Do you understand the difference between responding and reacting?

Reactions are automatic and robotic. They are instantaneous thoughts and actions that are triggered by personal programming and conditioning. These thoughts and actions are not divinely derived, but are, for the most part, ego-based and fear-driven. And they are usually accompanied by feelings of tension and anxiety.

A response, on the other hand, is based on the wisdom of your Spirit. It is not self-serving, but is always in the best interests of all involved. Even when time is of the essence, and a decision must be made quickly or an action must be taken immediately, when you are coming from Spirit you will still experience an underlying sense of peace.

A regular practice of meditation—especially in the early morning—is helpful because it enables you to stay more connected to your Spirit throughout the day. And because of that, you are better equipped to appropriately and effectively *respond* to situations, rather than rashly *react* to them. No matter how challenging a situation may be, you will be better able to sense what action—if any—is *divinely called for*.

This can be true even when you are in immediate physical danger, and you need to protect yourself. For example, on a road trip to Las Vegas in 2007, I suddenly noticed that a huge tire had flown off of an approaching truck, and the tire was now in my lane and hurtling straight at me! Instead of hastily reacting to the situation, I found myself actually taking the time to more accurately assess which way I should steer my car in order to avoid a collision . . . which—contrary to my first impression—turned out to be to the left. The entire incident only spanned a few seconds, but when you are open to the influence of your Spirit, that is more than enough time to make a more thoughtful choice.

If you want to experience life as an effortless flow of major and minor miracles, instead of an endless and arduous struggle, remember that—to a great degree—it is a matter of personal *responsibility*. That is to say, it is a matter of your *response ability*. Commit yourself to a daily practice of meditation, and you will find your ability to respond greatly enhanced, and your tendency to react greatly reduced. And that's a good thing. That's a God thing.

16

The Value of Meditation
Part 3

In the first two parts of my series on The Value of Meditation, I explained how meditation helps you intuitively sense divine direction, and how it helps you respond to challenging situations in a wiser way. In this message, I want to show you how meditation helps you maintain *present moment awareness*, which is also one of the main keys for living life in the divine flow.

If you are not familiar with meditation, you might assume that it's about mentally *escaping* the now moment. And yes, there are plenty of *guided* meditations that do, indeed, take you somewhere else in time and space. But strictly speaking, most *guided* meditations are really *visualizations*, which serve a different purpose.

The form of meditation that I recommend is specifically designed to center all of your attention in the *here and now*. How? First, by focusing your attention on your breathing (because your body is always in the present). And then, by focusing your attention on a mantra (a special phrase you repeat to yourself) to help displace your usual thoughts—the kind of thoughts that are likely to propel you elsewhere.

It's true, that after your meditation is over, it may be a challenge for you to *stay* in the present moment, and avoid drifting off into reflections on the past or projections into the future. But your *tendency* to do that will be greatly reduced, especially after a few weeks of practicing meditation consistently.

And the benefit of being more centered in the here and now? You will be much more aware of all the divine signs and synchronicities that are pointing you in a particular direction, and guiding you to your highest good. Remember that the *presence* of the flow is sensed in the *present*. You must be *here, now,* in order to see the divine signs. You must be *here, now,* in order to notice the divine synchronicities. And being *here, now,* is what meditation—as I practice it—helps you do.

17

The Value of Meditation
Part 4

In the first three parts of my series on The Value of Meditation, I described in detail how meditation helps you become more intuitive, more responsive, and more present. But the benefits of meditation don't stop there. There are, in fact, at least eight ways that meditation dramatically improves your experience of everyday life.

To conclude this series, here is a short summary of all eight ways that life is enhanced when—through a daily practice of meditation—you maintain contact with your inner Spirit:

1. **You are healthier.** Many health issues are either caused by, or aggravated by, stress. For the most part, stress comes from fearful thoughts. When you are in touch with your all-knowing, indestructible Spirit, fearful thoughts are either greatly diminished or completely removed.

2. **You are more creative.** True creativity comes from the Divine Creator within. When you are in touch with that Divine Creator, you automatically become more inspired.

3. **You are more intuitive.** When you are in touch with your inner Spirit, you can sense divine direction much more easily. So your next right step becomes much more obvious.

4. **You are more responsive.** Instead of hastily judging and rashly reacting to something unexpected in life, you calmly respond from the wisdom of your inner Spirit. You know what is best to do, when to do it, or if you should do anything at all.

5. **You are more present.** Your Spirit is always in the now moment. When you are in touch with your Spirit, you are less likely to be lost in thought—that is, reflecting on the past or projecting into the future. That means you are better able to notice the miracles that are happening all around you, right here, and right now.

6. **You are more patient.** Being in the eternal now, your Spirit never feels bound by time. And being all-knowing, your Spirit sees countless ways for you to move successfully through life. When you are in touch with your Spirit, possibilities seem unlimited, and time stands still. The result is infinite patience.

7. **You are more peaceful.** As an indestructible, eternal being, your Spirit knows nothing of fear, and it is always at peace. When you are in touch with that eternal, indestructible essence, you, too, will be at peace—no matter what is disturbing others.

8. **You are more loving.** Your Spirit is love itself—unconditional *divine* love. When you are in touch with your Spirit, you can't help but be more compassionate, understanding, accepting, and forgiving.

So, dear reader, I hope this series on meditation has increased your understanding of its practical value—of the benefits of going within, getting in touch with the Divine Spirit that resides there, and allowing that divine essence to express itself throughout the day. Meditation is, without a doubt, the single most powerful tool you have for enhancing your ability to be—and stay—"in the flow."

18

Manifesting Money

Would you like to make more money? If you are like most people, your answer to that question is probably a resounding "Yes!" The desire to "make more money" is one that is shared by almost everybody. But did you realize that dwelling on that desire could actually be *limiting* the abundance that you are experiencing in your life? Let's examine the desire to "make more money" for a moment, and see if it is something that you really want to focus on.

First of all, is *money* what you really want? Or is it an *experience* of comfort, security, adventure, or beauty that money can offer you?

As you know, I define the divine flow as an underlying current that is continually guiding you toward the effortless fulfillment of your heart's desires. But what your *heart* desires—what your *Divine Spirit* desires—is generally an *experience* of life. So that is what you should be focusing on—the *experience* that you want to have . . . not just *money*.

Money is not an experience. It is a means to an end. And in many cases, when you are following the divine flow, you will discover that money isn't even required to achieve your desire. Sometimes, the experience you desire is provided for you without cost at all! It comes to you freely, as a gift from the Universe.

One time, for example, I saw a painting of an angel that I really wanted—a painting that would satisfy my desire to experience more beauty in my life. The painting cost $400. And I was willing to pay that price. But through a series of unusual mistakes, I was never charged for the painting. I tried to settle the bill several times with both the credit card company and the online merchant who was selling the piece. But both companies insisted that I owed nothing, and that the painting was mine, free and clear. I felt like I had received a divine present.

And what about the idea that you want to *make* more money? Do you really want to *make* more money? Or do you just want to *have* more money?

The act of "making" often entails effort and struggle. When, instead, you focus on what it is you want to *experience,* any money that may be required to have that experience *flows to you naturally* as part of the manifestation process. Sometimes, you will receive money through miraculous channels like the ones I describe in my message titled, "The Flow of Abundance." More commonly, though, you will receive it through some kind of work that you do. When work is involved, it may look like you have undertaken that endeavor to "make money." But if you truly *enjoy* your work—and I hope you do—is making money your *main objective?* Or is making money the *beneficial result* of doing what you enjoy doing? Isn't it the latter?

So, dear reader, do you really want to "make more money?" Or, is your *true* desire to have some wonderful new *experiences*? If experiences are what you are after, then *focus* on that! Let the Universe know in no uncertain terms exactly what it is you want to *experience*. When you do that—when you focus on the *experiences* you want to have, rather than the *money* that may (or may not) be required to have those experiences—you will find your desires being fulfilled in a much more effective, efficient, and effortless manner.

19

Little Decisions
Can Make a Big Difference

Every decision that you make in life—no matter how small—can either enhance or restrict your experience of the divine flow in your life. Here's an example of a seemingly insignificant choice that Carol and I made, which resulted in something remarkable happening:

At the end of 2006, two women from Massachusetts—Beth and Cindi—felt divinely guided to attend an all-day event that would take place here in Sedona at the beginning of the new year. Before leaving home, they were talking to another friend of theirs, and they shared with her an experience they had which involved the song, "Row, Row, Row Your Boat." Well, this third person—Pat—happens to be an old friend of mine, and she informed Beth and Cindi that I had written a book with that title, and that I now live in Sedona.

Feeling inspired by this coincidence, Beth and Cindi decided they wanted to meet me while they were here. Pat put the three of us in touch, and I sent Beth and Cindi a note about how we could meet.

The plan was simple: Carol and I were going to be attending the very last part of the same event that Beth and Cindi were going to, so all they had to do was look for us when they came back from their dinner break. To make that possible, I sent them my picture.

When Carol and I got to the venue, we discovered that we had arrived early, and we had our choice of any two seats in the auditorium—an auditorium that holds 250 people. We carefully chose two particular seats, and patiently waited for Beth and Cindi to come up and introduce themselves.

About five minutes before the event was to resume—with the auditorium now completely full—two women finally approached me and asked, "Are you Steven?" It was Beth and Cindi. I said hello, and then I asked them if they had any trouble spotting me from my picture. Their amazing response was, "We didn't have a chance to look at your picture."

Puzzled, I asked, "Then how did you find me?" Beth and Cindi replied, "You and Carol happen to be sitting in the same two seats that we have been sitting in all day long. We just had a 'feeling' that it might be you." Wow! Out of 250 places to sit in that auditorium, Carol and I had chosen the exact two seats that Beth and Cindi had previously occupied!

The next day we spent the entire afternoon with Beth and Cindi. Suffice it to say that we all had remarkable gifts of healing and insight to share with each other, and it was an extremely meaningful experience for each of us.

The "moral" to this story? Well, like I said at the beginning of this message: Every decision that you make in life—no matter how small—can either enhance or restrict your experience of the divine flow in your life. *So choose with sensitivity.* Every little feeling that you have in life—no matter how illogical—can be an important guidepost for you. *So pay attention to that.*

Carol and I didn't just haphazardly choose our seats. We walked among dozens of seats and sat where we "felt" the most comfortable. And Beth and Cindi had absolutely no reason to think that the people sitting in their former seats were Carol and I, but they honored their intuitive feeling and acted on that guidance anyway.

Here are four people out of 250 that had the intention to meet, and the Universe brought us together flawlessly. But it only happened because Beth, Cindi, Carol, and I *cooperated* with that subtle orchestration. It makes me wonder just how effortless life would really be if we were *always* that sensitive to "the flow." Pretty darn effortless, I suspect!

20

Be True To Yourself

S hakespeare was a very wise man. Similar to the line I quoted at the start of my message titled, "The Constant Possibility of Good," here is another great line from Shakespeare's *Hamlet*: "To thine own self be true." When it comes to living life in the divine flow, that is especially good advice—on several levels.

For one, that statement reminds you to always be true to your *Higher Self*—that creative and loving Spirit that exists at the core of your being. There is no better way for you to be in the flow, than to get in touch with your own Divine Essence, and to let its wisdom lead the way.

"To thine own self be true" also reminds you to be true to who you are as a uniquely talented individual with a particular purpose in life. It almost goes without saying, that when you recognize what you are really passionate about, and you use your special gifts and abilities to express that passion, you will experience the flow like you have never experienced it before.

Finally, on a less lofty level, "To thine own self be true"

reminds you to honor all the little preferences you have in life—your likes and your dislikes—and to keep those preferences in mind as you try to discern your next right step.

It is always tempting to look at how other people achieve their goals and dreams, and want to follow in their footsteps. But the fact is, their path to success may not be well suited to you. Based on their interests and delights, as well as their talents and abilities, *their* flow may be completely different from *your* flow.

One thing I find fascinating about the divine flow is that it always seems to take your unique, individual nature into account. Yes, sometimes the flow may ask you to step slightly out of your comfort zone. But it will *not*—for any extended period of time—require you to engage in activities that are completely foreign to your personal makeup.

Think about it. Why would the flow—which knows you better than you know yourself—ask you to do something that you will probably say "no" to? With its infinite intelligence, wouldn't the flow take your personal preferences into account and orchestrate something that is "right up your alley?" Of course it would!

It may seem logical and reasonable for you to follow a path that seems to be working well for others—promoting a passion through Internet marketing and networking, for example. But if that kind of activity does not enliven you, or worse, if it actually seems to sap your spirit, the flow will *not* require that particular action of you. *Or,* the flow will present you with an "Earth Angel" who will take care of that action on your behalf.

Remember that living life in the divine flow is not about drifting. It is about taking action. But the action that you are required to take is *divinely guided* action. And that's the kind of action that always feels effortless—not just because it is *easy* to do, but because it is *divinely designed to be perfect for you!*

Here's to being true to *yourself,* and to always being faithful to *your* flow . . . and not to somebody else's.

21

Finding Good in Amarillo

In June of 2007 I drove my car from Sedona, Arizona to Overland Park, Kansas, to speak at two churches in that area, and to present my workshop at the annual conference of Unity churches.

I spent my first night on the road in a motel in Amarillo, Texas. When I got up the next morning and prepared to leave, I was shocked to discover that someone had broken through the rear window of my car, and several things had been stolen. Among the missing items was a box containing 46 copies of my first book. This box was unmarked, and there was no way for anyone to know what was in it.

That morning I was challenged to test the validity of two characteristics I believe to be true about the divine flow:

1. Everything that happens can be a stepping-stone to a higher good.

2. One person's good can never come at the expense of another's.

"Where (in the heck) is the higher good in this?" I asked myself. The answer to that first question came quickly. Right off the bat it occurred to me (and to almost everyone I spoke to about this incident), that there were now 46 copies of my book floating around Amarillo. Even if the entire box was immediately thrown into a dumpster, there are plenty of people in this world who search through dumpsters for things to sell, and—sadly—for something to eat. Some people even use them for a place to sleep.

Isn't it possible that at least *one* person in Amarillo has found my book, read it, and that his or her life is being changed for the better by it? Isn't it possible that this person would never have come across my book through any of the "normal" channels? I think that's entirely possible. Don't you? And isn't that a *good* thing? You bet it is!

But that brings up the second characteristic of the flow I mentioned. If someone is benefiting from my book, didn't that good come at *my expense*? Didn't I *lose* money as a result of my damaged car and missing items? In a word, no.

In talking to the insurance company, I was surprised to find out that the window in my car could be replaced with absolutely no cost to me. And even better, the cost of the items missing from my car was also covered.

Obviously, though, I lost precious time dealing with this circumstance—time that I really couldn't *afford to spend*. Right? Nope. This is where the story gets really interesting. You see, when I planned this particular trip, I thought it would take me three days to get where I was going. Once I reached Amarillo, however, I realized it was only going to take me *two* days to get there. As a result of my miscalculation, I had an entire day that was "free" for me to use in any way I wanted to, or needed to. I not only had plenty of time to deal with the police and the insurance company that morning, but that afternoon I had all the time I needed to find a place along my intended route that could replace my rear window on the spot!

That's right. When all was said and done, this situation didn't really cost me time *or* money. I arrived at my destination exactly when I thought I would, and I got there without any additional expense. I even had plenty of books to sell, because I brought three boxes of books with me, when—as it turned out—I only needed two!

Was I just incredibly lucky? Or was this a great example of the divine flow in action . . . a flow that always has the *highest good of everyone* in mind? I think the latter. How about you?

22

It's All Good! Or Is It?

In my message titled, "Finding Good In Amarillo," I wrote about a time when someone broke into my car at a motel, and stole—among other things—a box containing 46 copies of my first book. At first glance, this situation seemed "bad" for me. But it turned around so quickly and so effortlessly, it was easy to see the divine flow at work within it. Does that mean, though, that the incident *itself* was divinely orchestrated for someone's benefit?

In this case, I'd say that's possible. It seems a bit beyond chance that I just "happened" to have one more box of books in the car than I needed, and I just "happened" to have an extra day in my schedule to repair the car and continue my trip. That said, however, I don't believe that *everything* that happens in life that we tend to label as "bad," is actually good—that it is simply a divinely orchestrated "bend in the stream" that we are misjudging.

I, for one, believe in free will, which means that each and every one of us has the freedom to ignore or overrule the divine guidance that we are continually receiving. This guidance is always directing us to act in ways that are mutually beneficial for all. But when we are blind to that guidance, or when we dismiss it, there can be unfortunate consequences for ourselves, and for others, as well.

There are many people who love to say, "It's *all* good!" And I appreciate that positive attitude. I really do. But I think a more accurate statement would be this one: "It can all *lead* to good!" The wonderful thing about the divine flow is this: No matter what choices we make in life, or what the consequences of those choices are, there can always be a divine flow of good *from that point on!*

We live in an infinitely intelligent Universe. The Mind of the Divine can take any circumstance we may find ourselves in, and use that occurrence as a basis for the unfolding of something beneficial. But—and here's the main point of this particular message—for that to happen, it is up to us to *recognize* and *cooperate* with the unfolding of that good.

As long as we are blaming others or shaming ourselves for the "bad" situations we find ourselves in, our minds will not be open enough to receive the guidance that can lead us out of our predicament. As soon as things seem to be going awry, it is up to us to reaffirm that *everything can be a stepping-stone to a higher good* . . . if we want it to be. It is that kind of positive attitude that enables us to see the *opportunity for good* in every situation, and sense our next right step.

Here's to knowing that—regardless of the unguided decisions that we make, or the misguided actions that we take—the divine flow is always trying to create miracles out

71

of our mistakes. May we always be grateful for that. And may we always be mindful enough to *play our part* in that divine development.

23

Purposely Choosing Challenges

There is a logical conclusion that most people reach based on my definition of the divine flow. Again, that definition is: "An underlying current that is continually guiding you toward the effortless fulfillment of your heart's desires." From that statement you might conclude that if you are moving forward in life with a great deal of ease and grace, then you must be "in the flow." If, on the other hand, you keep running into unwanted challenges, then you are obviously "not in the flow."

Well, most of the time you would be absolutely right about that. As I mentioned in my last message—the one titled, "It's All Good. Or Is It?"—undesired circumstances are often the natural consequence of continually making choices that are contrary to divine direction. However, there will be plenty of times in life when a particular challenge you face *is*, indeed, *part* of the divine flow for you. How so?

For one, you have to remember that what you consider to be an unwanted challenge may not really be a challenge at all. It is simply the divine flow operating in a way that you just don't understand. Have you ever experienced a situation that you initially judged as "bad," only to have that situation transform on its own into something surprisingly beneficial? It pays to be open-minded about everything that occurs in life, and not judge circumstances too hastily. A little patience and acceptance on your part can help you experience an unwanted challenge as what it sometimes is—just a "bend in the stream" . . . a stream that is *still* helping you get where you want to go in the most beneficial way possible.

Other times, you may experience an unwanted challenge in life for quite a different reason: *It is actually the desire of your heart to experience that challenge!* That's right. Deep down inside, you actually *want* to experience that challenge, and the flow is simply providing that opportunity for you.

As I mention in my message titled, "Desires of the Heart," your heart is your Spirit, and your Spirit is in this life to have certain *experiences* of life. Most of those experiences are pleasant ones, such as love, abundance, and creative expression. Those are the kind of experiences that you *consciously know* you want to have, and look forward to having. However, there may also be some experiences that your Spirit knows you *need* that you are *not* consciously aware of. For instance, you may need healing from an emotional wound that has been buried for so long, you have almost forgotten that it is there. Or, you may need to be free from some kind of psychological conditioning that is causing you to limit your life in some manner.

Often, the best way to heal something from the *past,* or

grow beyond it, is through a *current* challenge. So the divine flow will *purposely* lead you to the perfect situation for growth or healing, even though that situation may seem to be unwanted.

For example, suppose you entered into a relationship that eventually turned out to be emotionally (or even physically) abusive. Obviously, that kind of relationship is not something that you would *consciously* choose to experience. But the reason the two of you were brought together might be very simple. It could well be that your current relationship is mirroring an abusive relationship that you experienced as a child. And the flow is giving you an opportunity to heal that wound—to finally stand up for yourself, reclaim your sense of inherent worth, and establish appropriate boundaries. As a child, you simply didn't have the wisdom, the words, or the power to do that.

So, whenever you encounter an unexpected challenge in life, don't jump to the conclusion that you are "not in the flow"—that you must be suffering the consequence of a misguided or unguided choice you made. It is entirely possible that you are merely misjudging the situation. Or, on a deeper, *unconscious* level, perhaps you are *choosing* to experience that particular challenge, and you are choosing it for a very good reason.

Just remember that no matter what is happening or why it is happening, everything can be a stepping-stone to your highest good. And what you are called upon to do is the same in every situation that seems undesirable: Stop blaming others or shaming yourself for creating that situation. Accept what is. And maintain a positive attitude, so you will be open and receptive to your next divinely guided step.

Who knows, that step may be one that leads you to a long-overdue emotional healing, the lifting of a self-imposed limitation, or maybe just an opportunity for you to learn a very valuable life lesson.

24

The Therapeutic Effect
of Non-Resistance

Many, many moons ago, when I was in my late twenties, I suffered from chronic lower back pain. And "suffered" is the right word to use here. Because, over time, that pain became so intense, it was almost paralyzing.

Seeking the source of my problem, I consulted my family physician, an orthopedic surgeon, an internist, a chiropractor, and an arthritis specialist. Although tests revealed that I was definitely experiencing some kind of severe inflammation, not a single one of those medical professionals was able to diagnose my condition.

One day, with no relief in sight, and nowhere else to turn, I sat down, threw up my hands, and basically said to myself, "Oh, to *heck* with it!" I gave up trying to fight the pain, and just surrendered to it. And guess what? Almost immediately, the pain began to subside. And within a week or so, it was completely gone.

I was pain-free for several months, and then the pain returned. But this time, I responded to it differently. Instead of resisting the pain, I simply observed it. "Oh, there's that pain again," I said to myself. As uncomfortable as it was, I accepted the pain. And this time, it went away in a matter of days.

It was a year before the pain came back again. And when it did, once again I didn't resist it. I just allowed it to be. And once again, it quickly passed. And that's when I had an epiphany about the pain I was experiencing. Although the pain was very real, and there was probably a very real reason I was experiencing inflammation in that part of my body, I realized that *it was my resistance to the pain* that caused it to increase in intensity and severity.

The original pain itself was not really intolerable. But when I *resisted* the pain, my body would become so tense, the pain was greatly magnified. And the longer I resisted the pain, the more chronic my condition became. The "cure" was for me to "relax into the pain," and make it easier for my body to do what it is designed to do—heal itself. My resistance—and the tension and anxiety that accompanied that resistance—was only creating a toxic environment that inhibited my body's natural healing response.

In short, I discovered the therapeutic effect of non-resistance. Several years passed before I had to deal with that pain again. And it has now been well over two decades since I have experienced that particular issue.

There is a popular saying that goes like this: "What you resist, persists." And you can certainly see how that applies to this situation. But there is another saying that is equally apropos: "Suffering is optional." That statement refers to the fact that a certain amount of pain may be inescapable in life, but *suffering* is experiencing that pain to an *exaggerated extent,* and—in many cases—that degree of pain is avoidable.

Dear reader, whether you are *physically* suffering due to an illness or an injury, or you are *emotionally* suffering because of a hurtful situation or a seemingly detrimental circumstance, I encourage you to practice non-resistance to see if it lessens the severity of your pain. Allow yourself to feel your pain *just as it is,* instead of fighting against the very *existence* of your pain—which, of course, is futile. What is . . . *is!* All the resistance in the world is not going to alter that fact. And your resistance may actually be making the experience worse.

Here's to the therapeutic effect of non-resistance! Here's to knowing that sometimes the best thing you can do to help alleviate your suffering is to just sit down, throw up your hands, and say to yourself, "Oh, to *heck* with it!"

Note: If you have any reason at all to suspect that you have a truly serious physical or emotional condition, please don't hesitate to immediately seek the counsel of a certified health professional. Non-resistance may lessen the severity of your pain, but it may not eliminate your pain altogether, or remove its cause.

25

On Health and Healing

In my previous message titled, "The Therapeutic Effect of Non-Resistance," I described how it is possible to reduce the severity of any pain that you may be experiencing by allowing yourself to feel your pain *just as it is* . . . instead of *resisting* it. Sometimes, it is your resistance to pain that causes it to increase in intensity and become unbearable.

However—as I pointed out at the very end of that message—non-resistance may lessen the severity of your pain, but it might not eliminate it altogether, or remove its cause. This is especially true with a serious physical condition. And that is why I also recommend seeking the assistance of a certified health professional. That said, though, is there anything that you—*yourself*—can do to help heal a physical problem at its source? Yes, there is. Here are three suggestions:

First, affirm in your mind what you Know to be True in your heart: that your body is already working to cure your illness or repair your injury. Remember that your body is continually in the healing mode, and—within certain limits— it is a very powerful healer all by itself. The main thing that slows down that natural healing process is stress. When you consciously affirm the healing power of your body—and are grateful for that—the peace and comfort you feel helps ease the tension within your body, and creates a relaxed environment that is more conducive to healing.

Second, enhance your body's healing response through the power of visualization. A number of years ago, I created a visualization that continues to be particularly effective for me. In a light state of meditation, I picture my True Body as a Body of Light—a translucent, three-dimensional, "spiritual blueprint" of my body. Then I imagine my *material* body continually attempting to *match* that spiritual blueprint—removing what is *not* on the blueprint, and restoring what *is* on it. Don't underestimate the power of visualization. I once developed a small cyst on my thumb, and a much larger one on my scalp. But both completely disappeared in a matter of weeks when I spent some time each morning visualizing the healing process I just described.

Finally, make sure that you are being completely open and receptive to divine guidance—the kind of guidance that may lead you to something else that is essential for your healing. Through divine signs, synchronicities, or people who appear in your path, you may be divinely directed to an alternative health professional, or guided to a particular kind of medicinal herb. Or, through your own intuitive sense, you may become aware of some other way that you can directly promote your recovery, such as changing your diet or revising your exercise regimen. Remember, though, if you want to be truly open and receptive to divine counsel, it necessary to maintain a present and positive state of mind . . . and, yes, that can be somewhat of a challenge—especially if your illness or injury is particularly distracting or disturbing.

Regardless of how you are divinely guided in your healing—whether you are directed to consult a traditional medical specialist, led to an acupuncturist or homeopathic healer, inspired to alter your diet, or guided to pursue any combination of these things and more—keep in mind that every health challenge can offer you some kind of gift. Your illness or injury may help you live a more balanced life by reminding you of what is truly important in this world. Or, it may simply serve to renew your appreciation for the gift of good health. Whatever challenge you face, I invite you to look for the blessing in it.

Here's to your health, your healing, and your wholeness.

26

Your Creative Spirit

L ike most people in the world, I was deeply saddened by
the premature passing of Steve Jobs, co-founder of Apple
Computers. Not since the death of John Lennon have I felt
this kind of loss. It reminded me how much I value creative
expression, and how much I admire those who tap into that
inner source of pure inspiration, and pursue their dreams with
both passion and patience.

There are those who point out that Steve Jobs was best
at improving products that already existed. Perhaps so. But
the innovations he introduced went way beyond tweaks and
nudges. He had a way of looking at commonplace things like
phones and music players and seeing their possibilities in
radically new and inventive ways.

I think Steve Jobs is a wonderful example of how
creative we can be, inspiring each of us to live our lives to
their fullest creative potential. What's that you say? You're
not creative? I beg to differ. As an individual expression of
what many call "The Great Creator," you are—at the *heart*
of your being—nothing less than a Divine Creator in your

own right. Creativity is as much a part of your innate nature as love is.

You don't have to be an author, a painter, a musician, or an inventor to express your divinely creative nature. Everything in life can be used as a creative outlet. Whether you are decorating a house, raising a family, landscaping a yard, or developing a new business, nothing satisfies the soul more than creating something new in this world that didn't exist before.

The challenge is letting go of all those limiting thoughts about yourself—and your perceived potential—that inhibit your creativity. Remember that your combination of talents, gifts, and abilities is unlike anyone else's, and you have something unique to contribute to this world in a way that absolutely nobody else can. Your job is to quiet your mind long enough to hear that inner creative Spirit that speaks to you through your intuition, and blesses you with divine ideas, insights, and inspiration. To quote Steve Jobs, himself:

> "Your time is limited, so don't waste it living someone else's life. Don't be trapped by dogma—which is living with the results of other people's thinking. Don't let the noise of other's opinions drown out your own inner voice. And most importantly, have the courage to follow your heart and intuition. They somehow already know what you truly want to become. Everything else is secondary."

27

An Easter Reminder

As the saying goes, "You are not a human being having an occasional spiritual experience. You are a spiritual being having a temporary human experience." And there is no better time of the year to affirm that for yourself than Easter.

For me, the Easter story is a dramatic demonstration and profound illustration of something that I believe is just as true for *you* now, as it was for Jesus over 2,000 years ago—that you are *in* this world, but you are not *of* this world.

Like I often mention, your *true essence* is Spirit, not body. And unlike the body, your Spirit is eternal and indestructible. Your *authentic self* is, in a word, *divine*—an individual expression of that source energy that many of us call God. And you are here for one purpose, and one purpose only: to express your divine nature in the body, and in the world.

And what, exactly, *is* that nature? Love. *Unconditional* love. *Divine* love. It's the kind of love that knows no limits—the kind of love that forgives *no matter what*. It's the kind of love that Jesus fully expressed throughout his life, right up to the final moments of his earthly existence. And it's the kind of love that you, and I, and *all* of us are called upon to express on a daily basis.

Today, and *every* day of the year, may you remember who you are, and why you are here. May you remember that the journey of life is not about *getting somewhere*. The journey of life is about *being something*. It's about being the love that you are in every single moment of that journey. And it's about experiencing the absolute joy that your love brings to the journey, and brings to each and every Spirit that you encounter along the way.

28

Divine Procrastination

Have you ever had something on your "To Do List" that you knew was important for fulfilling a particular desire, but—for some reason—you kept putting off doing it? Then, one day, you just *suddenly* felt like taking that action? And when you did, you discovered that your timing was absolutely perfect, and everything flowed beautifully? I've had that happen quite a bit. And I've coined a phrase for it. I call it "Divine Procrastination."

As a rule, procrastination is not constructive. But occasionally, there's a very good reason why you don't feel like doing something. Your inner Spirit is telling you that the timing just isn't right!

Sometimes, your part of the manifestation process needs to be delayed until other pieces of the puzzle are put into place—until other people do what they are being divinely directed to do, or obstacles that you are unaware of are removed from your path.

Sometimes, too, you may not feel motivated to act, because your Spirit knows that it would be premature for you to accomplish a particular goal right now. There might be a few things that you need to learn first.

Or, if you have a dream to bring a brand new product or service into this world, perhaps your Spirit knows that your product or service will be much easier to produce or provide at a later date, or maybe the additional time will give you the opportunity to make your offering an even better one.

That said, please don't use this idea of divine procrastination as a flimsy excuse for continually dragging your feet, or for avoiding something that is outside of your personal comfort zone. You'll know when you are doing that, because you will feel a subtle sense of guilt about your procrastination, instead of feeling perfectly okay about it. Just be aware that, on any given day, some things on your "To Do List" will elicit more positive and peaceful feelings than others. *And pay attention to that.*

Rest assured, that when the time is right, your Spirit will give you the nudge you need. *All of a sudden* you will just *feel* like taking a step that may have been on your list for days, weeks, or even months.

What's on your "To Do List" right now? Is there something that seems to stand out today, that didn't yesterday? Is there a subtle sense of "rightness" about doing something in particular on your list, or a new sense of urgency about it? Perhaps your Spirit is trying to tell you something. Perhaps the day has come for you to finally take that action that you have been putting off for quite some time.

29

Divine Signs
Part I

Although your own intuition is the most valuable, reliable, and consistent source of divine guidance you have, there are many other vehicles that the Universe uses to communicate with you. If you are open and receptive, awake and aware, you will see "divine signs" all around you.

Sometimes these divine signs will show you the next right step you need to take to fulfill a particular dream or desire. Other times they may inform you of something important that you need to know. What fascinates me the most is this: Quite often, those divine signs are *literal* signs—that is, they are actual printed messages on a poster, a wall, or some other surface!

If you have already read *Row, Row, Row Your Boat,* you may recall that I was divinely guided to my publisher through a series of events that included a billboard I saw on the side of the highway. What a divine sign that turned out to be . . . and a very *big* sign, at that!

Here's another example: This sign was given to Anne, a woman I met when I spoke at her church in Flagstaff, Arizona.

Anne told me that at one point in her life she was thinking about making a decision that would alter her future dramatically. It was such a radical change, she had a lot of fear about making that choice, and she spent many long days (and many sleepless nights) wondering if her life would really be better by making that move. It would certainly be easier and safer for her to not take any action at all, and stick with the life she knew. But what if she reached the end of her life, and she was *still wondering* what her life *could* have been like? Wouldn't that be worse than going ahead and taking the risk? Wouldn't it be worse to die wondering?

Finally, one morning, Anne woke up and went downstairs into her living room. There, sitting on the couch, was one of her son's friends. And guess what was printed on that young man's T-shirt? Incredibly, it was these three words: "DON'T DIE WONDERING!"

Wow! Needless to say, that was just the divine sign that Anne needed to help her make her decision. As she told me, "It was just a message on a T-shirt, but it propelled me into action in an astonishing way." Anne made her choice—a choice for change—and she has no regrets to this day.

To quote my favorite saying: "There's God. And There's Not Paying Attention." Pay attention, dear reader, and you *will* receive the divine direction you are seeking. In fact, it may be *literally* spelled out for you on a billboard, a bumper sticker . . . or even a T-shirt. What a blessing it is to know that we can be so *clearly* guided!

30

Divine Signs
Part 2

In the first part of this series on Divine Signs, I focused on
the kind of divine signs that are *literal*—that is, actual
words that have been printed or painted on a surface somewhere. These literal signs are so succinct and so direct, they
are often as amusing as they are amazing. For example, you
might be wondering whether you should take a certain step or
not, and there on the car in front of you is a Nike bumper
sticker that says, "Just Do It!"

Of course, we also receive divine signs that are *not*
literal. They are *figurative*—that is, they are objects, animals,
or insects to which *we ourselves* have assigned special
meaning. Usually, we assign meaning to certain objects,
animals, or insects, because something very beneficial
occurred when one of those things was present, or something
significant happened immediately after its appearance. Then—
at another time or in another place—the same unusual
juxtaposition happened again.

From that moment on, when those things show up in
our lives, we know that we are receiving a divine sign of some

kind, and we take heed. As I mentioned in Part 1, we might become aware of the next step we need to take to accomplish a goal or realize a dream. Or, we might have a flash of insight that helps us understand something better, or even helps us heal an emotional wound.

Please make sure, though, that you are not assigning meaning to something too hastily. If it is *truly* a divine sign, it will usually have these two characteristics:

1. The object, animal, or insect itself will be very unusual; or, it will be something ordinary that is showing up at an extraordinary time or place; or, it will be something that is highly personal to you, and to you alone. It is wise to avoid assigning meaning to common, everyday things that are likely to appear in your life on a frequent basis.

2. *Every* time this sign appears, something helpful happens. Divine signs are consistently beneficial. If you are experiencing mixed results, the divine nature of that sign is questionable.

Here's a great example of a divine sign that arrived in the unlikely form of an opossum: In 2007 one of my oldest and dearest friends was devastated when her daughter died suddenly and unexpectedly while she was in college. That kind of tragic event can shake almost anyone's faith, and my friend was no exception. She began to question everything she thought she believed. Does life *really* continue after death? *Really*? Does the soul *truly* live on? Does consciousness actually survive? Or do we simply cease to exist in every way, shape, and form?

Month after month these questions plagued my friend. At times she would be certain of life's continuity, but at other times, doubtful. She desperately wanted to believe that even though her daughter was no longer embodied, her Spirit was very much alive, and only the physical nature of their relationship had changed.

Then, one day, my friend noticed an opossum lying very still in her backyard. She had lived in this house for decades, and had never seen an opossum in her yard before. As she approached the creature, it seemed to be near death. It was breathing, but very, very slowly. So she gingerly picked it up, and moved it into the alley behind her house.

After a while, my friend went back to the alley to check on the animal. At this point, there were no signs of life whatsoever. No detectable breath. Nothing. My friend concluded that the animal must have died. And, with great respect and reverence, she laid the stiff and lifeless body to rest.

A few weeks later, the exact same thing happened again. Another opossum was lying motionless in her backyard. Amazed and confused, my friend once again moved the barely-breathing creature to the alley. But this time, she got on the Internet to do a little research on opossums. And she found out what you probably already know: When opossums feel threatened, they mimic all the appearances of being dead. Their lips curl back. They become very rigid. They even emit a "death smell." And they can remain that way for hours.

After my friend got off the computer, she went back to the alley to check on the creature. This time, the opossum was gone. Apparently, it was neither dead nor dying. It had simply *looked* that way. That's when my friend realized that she had been given a gift—a divine sign to help heal her heavy heart. The opossums were a symbolic reminder—and confirmation—that even though our bodies may become lifeless, death is really just an "appearance." Our *true nature* lives on.

My friend needed a sign to help her know—on a very deep level—that her daughter's Spirit is, indeed, *eternal* . . . that her daughter's essence can *never* die or disappear. And just to make sure that my friend really got the message, a *third* opossum soon showed up at her home. This opossum, however, was obviously alive and well—big and fat and helping itself to some cat food on my friend's front porch.

I find the progression of this story remarkable. When my friend assumed that the *first* opossum was dead—and treated it as such—a *second* one came and helped her look *beyond* appearances. And then a *third* opossum showed up, so what was once troubling my friend in the "backyard" of her mind, was replaced by a sign of life on the "front porch" of her mind.

So, dear reader, were these opossums *truly* a "divine sign" for my friend? Or was their appearance in her yard just a chance happening? You can draw your own conclusion. But I'm pretty sure you know what I believe . . . especially if you have already read my message titled, "Transformation."

31

Divine Signs
Part 3

In the first two parts of this series on Divine Signs, I described two different types of divinely meaningful messages—the *literal* kind, which appear as words or phrases on everything from billboards to bumper stickers; and the *figurative* kind, which appear in the form of personally significant objects, animals, or insects. To conclude this series, I want to explore one more kind of divine sign—the kind of sign that you have probably experienced on numerous occasions. I'm talking about the occurrence of a "meaningful coincidence."

I don't mean the kind of coincidence that *directly* helps you fulfill a certain desire, or complete a step that you know you need to take . . . like when you run into someone you haven't seen in ages, and each of you just "happens" to have exactly what the other one needs. That kind of coincidence is a miracle in and of itself. And you'll find lots of stories in this book about just that kind of synchronistic event . . . like the amazing story I share in my message titled, "Divine Encounters."

Instead, in this message I want to focus on the kind of coincidence that simply "tells" you something that is helpful—something that confirms an intuitive inkling that you have, or helps you make a decision about taking (or not taking) a particular step. It's the kind of coincidence that—when it happens—your very first thought is likely to be: "It's a sign!"

Like most divine signs, a meaningful coincidence will usually have a very uplifting and positive nature about it. But even seemingly "negative" signs can also prove to be valuable. Here's an example of that:

When Carol and I decided to move from Dallas, Texas to Sedona, Arizona, we felt a deep and abiding sense of peace about that choice, and doors began to open for us immediately. We truly felt that we were being divinely supported in our decision.

Nevertheless, moving to Arizona did involve quite a few risks. So, at times, Carol and I continued to entertain the idea of staying in Dallas for a little while longer. And that's when we began to get some helpful signs of a very different nature. Suddenly, various reasons that we had for *remaining* in Dallas began to deteriorate.

For one, we had been living in a luxurious, townhouse-style apartment that we absolutely loved. The price was right, the water was free, and our pristine, white wooden balcony gave the whole place a wonderful, warm, homey feel. But suddenly, both our building and our balcony were painted a drab color that we didn't like; for the first time in years, our rent was raised by $60 a month; and we began to be charged for water and trash pick-up, as well. All of a sudden, our perfect little nest wasn't so perfect.

Then Carol experienced a similarly disturbing downturn at her place of business. Her working conditions had been wonderful, and her earning potential even better. But suddenly, the company put a cap on Carol's base salary, and adopted some policies that made it much more difficult for her to earn commissions. To say the least, Carol was not happy about that.

Were these changes *truly* divine signs encouraging Carol and me to go ahead and make the move? All I know for sure is this: The sudden and unexpected occurrence of those changes, combined with their coincidental timing, certainly made it a whole lot easier for us to leave Dallas.

So, dear reader, whenever you wonder if a course of action that you are considering taking is divinely supported or not, pay attention to the signs that crop up—*all* the signs. Some signs may be literal. Some may be figurative. And some may come in the form of occurrences that are significant in light of their synchronistic timing and/or surrounding circumstances.

Whatever kind of signs you receive, I encourage you to take the time to discern the message those signs may have for you, and make the move you feel you are being divinely directed to make.

32

Imaginary Troubles

In September of 2007, I spoke at a Unity church in the charming old town of Quincy, Illinois. Quincy is only twenty miles from Hannibal, Missouri, the boyhood home of Mark Twain. When I discovered that fact, I was reminded of my favorite quote by Mark Twain:

> "I have known a great many troubles in my life.
> But most of them never happened."

Have you ever spent hours fretting and worrying about some kind of problem that—at that particular point in time—had *yet* to occur . . . and that you had no totally reliable way of knowing that it actually *would* occur? I certainly have. And sometimes, I still do. I foresee some potential "trouble" looming ahead of me, and then I start imagining *in great detail* what it will be like to live through that challenge.

What a misuse of the imagination that is! And just think of the unnecessary stress that puts on the body, because the body doesn't always know the difference between an *imagined* experience and a *real* one! When you are having an experience in your mind, then you might as well be truly living it!

Perhaps, if you could predict an event with 100% accuracy, then there might be some kind of benefit in letting it play out in your head. But most of the time—if not *all* of the time—you simply cannot forecast what is going to happen in your life. Life is always full of surprises. So it doesn't make much sense to continually imagine the worst. And when you do, you are not only needlessly torturing yourself, but you are also blocking your ability to be in the flow. How so?

Well, for one, to be in the flow you must be *open* and *receptive* to divine direction, and that requires a *positive* frame of mind. Any kind of negativity—including the kind of waking nightmares I am describing here—will greatly interfere with your ability to see the divine signs and sense the intuitive nudges that are guiding you to your good.

Also, projecting yourself into the future takes your attention off of the present. And guess what? The present is where the flow is—not the future. *Now* is when the flow opens doors for you. And *now* is when the flow creates opportunities for you. If you want to live your life in the divine flow, you must be aware, awake, and alive in the *present* moment. Only in the *current* moment can you sense that underlying *current* of celestial assistance, and take advantage of it.

Isn't life challenging enough without making stuff up? Instead of jumping ahead and experiencing "troubles" that have *yet* to happen, and may *never* happen, why not focus on what actually *is* happening. It's the only thing that is *ever* happening—the here and now moment. You may be amazed by the incredible peace and power you find there.

33

On Subconscious
Self-Sabotage

Oddly enough, although you may think that you are doing everything you should do to manifest your goals and dreams in life, you may be making some choices that—to an outside observer—are obviously *sabotaging* your ability to achieve those goals and dreams. Now why in the world would you do that?

One answer is because you may be harboring a few *subconscious beliefs* that are influencing your decisions in a counter-productive way. You may tell yourself that you want to have a fulfilling relationship, but somewhere along the line you may have come to deeply believe that "all relationships are doomed to failure." You may tell yourself that you want a wonderful job, but at an early age you may have firmly decided that "good things only happen to *other* people."

To one extent or another, we all allow subconscious beliefs such as these to govern our choices, and we end up undermining ourselves. For example, I once met a man who claimed that he wanted to make more money, and he had some inspired ways to do that. He had come up with several unique services that could easily attract a large number of paying customers. And yet, time after time, I saw this man make choices that made it almost impossible for people to know about his services, and to take advantage of what he was offering. And so, each of his endeavors failed.

I was very puzzled by this pattern—and so was he—until one of this man's most deeply held beliefs finally came to light. It was the belief that "you can't be *both* spiritual *and* prosperous." This man wasn't about to allow himself to become successful! Why? Because above all, he wanted to be spiritual! So he would repeatedly make choices that sabotaged his ability to make money.

Think for a minute, dear reader . . . have you noticed a repeating pattern in your life that is not serving you well? You know the kind of pattern I am talking about, right? It's the kind where you usually say to yourself, "Why is this always happening to me?" A recurring issue like that is often a sign that you are harboring a subconscious belief that is causing you to make certain decisions that are self-defeating. But since that belief is one that you are not *consciously* aware of, what can you do about it?

Well, you are on the right track by asking yourself the question, "Why is this always happening to me?" You are probably sincere in wanting to know—and fix—whatever is causing this issue to come up over and over again. The problem with that question is the portion of it that says, "to me." If something is happening *to you*—if the world is doing it *to you*, or God is doing it *to you*—how are you going to change that? Change the world? Change God? You know that won't work. So what *will* work?

Believe it or not, one thing you can do to help heal or eliminate a recurring issue is to simply turn your question around. Don't ask, "Why is this always happening to me?" Instead, say, "I must *want* that experience . . . but why would I?" I know it sounds simplistic, but when you put the question that way, you are doing two very important things:

First, by being open the idea that—at some level—you actually *want* to experience what you are experiencing, you free yourself from the helpless mentality of a victim. Taking full responsibility for what you experience in life helps you *regain your power* to make different and more constructive choices.

Second, your *willingness* to find the answer within *yourself* is sometimes all it takes to bring long-forgotten beliefs into the light. Once brought into the light, the false, simplistic, and childish nature of many of these beliefs is obvious, and they can often be quickly dispelled.

I am not claiming that this approach—"I must *want* that experience . . . but why would I?"—is a magical fix for every issue that occurs in your life. I just know that it has worked for me on several occasions, revealing and healing false beliefs I had about life that developed way back in my early childhood.

Try it. It's one simple thing you can do to break free from beliefs that may be holding you back from fulfilling your heart's desires. It's one simple step you can take to restore your ability to make choices that are *truly aligned* with your goals and dreams.

Note: Not *every* recurring issue in your life is the result of a subconscious belief that is negatively influencing your decisions. Sometimes, you may experience a repeating challenge in your life because your Spirit knows that you *need* that experience in order to heal or grow in some way. For more about that, I encourage you to read my message titled, "Purposely Choosing Challenges."

34

Consciously
Limiting Yourself

In my preceding message titled, "On Subconscious Self-Sabotage," I focused on *subconscious* beliefs that prevent you from achieving your goals and dreams in life, because they influence your choices in a counter-productive way. It is not uncommon, however, to also harbor *conscious* beliefs that are equally self-defeating—beliefs about yourself that limit your ability to live an abundant, fulfilling life. Here is a little example of that:

In June of 2006 I conducted a workshop at a church in Oklahoma City. At one point I called out a set of numbers, which I asked participants to add up in their heads. The numbers were easy. I called them out slowly. And I repeated the series twice, giving participants two chances to arrive at the correct total. But even then, *half* of the participants *still* got the total wrong—not just once, but *both* times. The point of this exercise was to demonstrate that you must take everything you think you "know" with a giant grain of salt—even something that you have thought through very, very carefully.

After the workshop was over, one woman came up to me and shared a revelation she had during that particular portion of my presentation. She told me that when I explained what we were going to do, her immediate thought was, "I can't do that. I don't do numbers." But since we had spent the first hour of the workshop talking about self-sabotaging beliefs, she became aware that this idea of "I can't do that" might be a self-imposed restriction . . . and a limitation that she was applying to more areas of her life than just math.

For the first time in her life, this woman was willing to consider the possibility that this limiting belief—no matter what its origin may have been—*was not necessarily true.* So she decided to momentarily let go of that belief, and she allowed herself to participate in the exercise.

And guess what? She not only got the total right, but she got it right the first time through—something that very few of my workshop participants ever do! She amazed herself. And right then and there, her perception about herself and her abilities changed for the better.

Dear reader, what do you tell yourself that might be inhibiting your ability to live life to its fullest? Are you absolutely certain that it is true? Or is it possible that you are unnecessarily limiting yourself?

I invite you to let go of what you "know" about yourself, and—in so doing—open yourself up to a whole new realm of possibility.

35

Motherhood and Manifesting

Here in the United States, the second Sunday in May is Mother's Day. That's the day we celebrate the women in our lives who conceived us, gave birth to us, and nurtured us as we began to establish our own individual identities in the world.

As I contemplate the beauty of motherhood on this special day, I can't help but notice the similarity between motherhood and manifesting. What similarity, exactly?

Well, as I have mentioned in several of these messages, you are an innately creative being. No matter how happy and fulfilled you are, you will always be *conceiving* of things you want to have, do, or be in your life. Through your words and your actions you will constantly be *giving birth* to your ideas—to your dreams, goals, and desires. And by giving them your love and attention, you will continually be in the process of *nurturing* your creations—of helping them grow into full expression.

In other words, whether you are male or female, whether you have brought a child into this world or not, in many respects you are—at the center of your being—a mother . . . someone who is divinely designed to bring something new and beautiful into this world.

As you pay tribute to your mother (or mothers), and to all the mothers living in the world *around* you, I invite you to take a moment to also honor the mother that exists *within* you. Take a moment to celebrate that motherly part of you that is an open chamber for receiving divine ideas, and an open channel for bringing those beautiful ideas into the world, and giving them life.

Here's to the joy of motherhood! And here's to the peace that comes from knowing that the whole Universe is willing to help you with that wonderful and immensely fulfilling work.

36

The Wisdom of Not Acting

In many of these messages, I encourage you to constantly attune yourself to the flow so you can discern your next right step—so you can intuitively sense what action you are being divinely guided to take. Sometimes, however, the best action that you can take is to do nothing at all. There is great wisdom in knowing when to stop what you are doing, get out of the way, and give the flow some time to work its magic on your behalf.

I still remember one of the first times I put my faith in the divine flow and consciously chose *not* to act. It was a day when I had been accidentally scheduled to be in three different business meetings all at the same time. My initial reaction was to jump on the phone and immediately try to change everyone's schedule around. However, when I took a minute to quietly "sense" my next right step, I got a strong feeling that the best thing for me to do was to simply go get a cup of coffee. That's it. Just go get a cup of coffee, and do nothing right at that moment to rectify the problem.

So that's exactly what I did. And guess what? When I

got back to my desk, my secretary informed me that one person had called to cancel their appointment, and another had called to move our meeting to a different time. During the five minutes that I was away, everything had worked itself out perfectly—without my help. In fact, if I *had* taken immediate action, I would only have interfered with the process and further complicated the situation.

Please understand, I am certainly not suggesting that you just "drift" through life by taking one, long, endless coffee break. I am only reminding you that "rowing with the flow" is not about *constant activity*. When you attune yourself to the flow, sometimes the next right step that you will be divinely directed to take will be to take *no action* at all.

As you row your boat down the stream toward your dream, don't forget to *pause* between each and every stroke of your oars to continually attune yourself to the flow. And if the flow directs you to pause a little longer than usual . . . so be it! You will know it's for the best.

37

When The Flow Seems Slow

I am happy to say that most of the time, I can sense the divine flow in my life quite easily. I notice a steady stream of signs, synchronicities, and intuitive nudges that are all pointing me in one particular direction. And when I head in that direction, I feel like I am in a gently moving current that is helping me get where I want to go with effortless ease.

Sure, sometimes there are unexpected twists and turns along the way. But usually, those surprising detours quickly transform into stepping-stones to a higher good. So even in those circumstances, I can still sense the divine flow at work on my behalf. In other words, whether the flow takes a direct route, or a more circuitous one, some kind of divine movement in my life is usually very apparent. But not always.

Occasionally, I experience periods in my life when it feels like the flow is hardly moving at all, leaving me in still waters for days—or even weeks—on end. I do not see any signs, or experience any meaningful coincidences. Doors are not opening for me. Opportunities are not presenting themselves. My inner voice is silent. And I have no idea what my next right step is.

Dear reader, are you experiencing a dramatically slow flow in your life right now? Then I invite you to consider the following:

- The flow may be slowing things down on purpose, so you will arrive at just the right place at just the right moment. It's simply a matter of divine timing.

- The flow may be hard at work removing obstacles in your path that you are not aware of.

- Because of certain freewill decisions that you—or others—have made, the flow may be rearranging a lot of things, so you can once again move forward in the most beneficial way possible.

- The flow may simply be giving you the time to become the kind of person you need to be *before* you arrive at your chosen destination.

Those are just a few of the reasons why the flow can seem painfully slow at times. The challenge in those trying times is to not lose your patience. You may feel like there is something that you should be doing to bring you one step closer to your chosen destination, and doing nothing feels uncomfortable. But, as I mentioned in my preceding message titled, "The Wisdom of Not Acting," in many instances doing nothing is exactly what is called for.

Sometimes, your job is just to wait patiently while the divine flow works its magic. And that's when it is more important than ever for you to meditate on a daily basis. Why? Because meditation helps you become more patient.

When you meditate you are consciously connecting with your inner Divine Spirit—that part of you that lives in a world beyond time and space. Your Spirit is always in the Eternal Now, which means that how long something is going to take, or how far away something is, are meaningless concepts. What may try the patience of your ego is never, ever, an issue for your Spirit.

Remember too, that your Spirit can see a virtually unlimited number of ways for you to achieve your dream. So when something occurs that blocks your way or impedes your progress, your ego may become impatient, but your Spirit won't.

If you want to avoid frustration—and the unpleasant consequences that can come from losing your patience and *forcing* your way forward—take some time each morning to consciously connect with that all-knowing, eternal Spirit within you . . . a Spirit that is, by its very nature, infinitely patient. And the rest of the time? Hey, enjoy the break! Take care of all the little details in life that are calling for your attention. Enjoy the time that you have been given to partake of life's many simple pleasures. And take advantage of this opportunity to just "be."

Don't worry about how slow the flow may seem. If—through your daily practice of meditation—you remain open and receptive to divine direction, I assure you that the current will pick up soon enough. Eventually, clear guidance *will* come. Your next divinely directed step *will* appear. And helpful doors *will* open. And when that happens, there is a very good chance that you will be able to see the perfect timing in it all.

38

Grow With The Flow

In my last message—the one titled, "When The Flow Seems Slow"—I said that sometimes the flow will slow down because it is giving you the time to become the kind of person you need to be *before* you arrive at your chosen destination. That's an important point, and I think it deserves further explanation. So here goes:

If you have a grand dream that you are pursuing, that doesn't mean that you are fully equipped to handle its manifestation at this particular moment in time. If you arrive at your destination prematurely, you might not be able to remain there very long . . . or even be able to enjoy it.

At a minimum, there may be some skills that you need to develop before your dream is fully realized. Have you ever looked back on your life and noticed how certain skills that you acquired along the way served you wonderfully later on?

Even more importantly, you may have some personal issues that need to be addressed before it is wise—or even possible—for your desire to be fulfilled. There may be some emotional wounds that need to be healed. There may be some self-sabotaging behaviors that need to be revealed. There may be some mental conflicts that need to be resolved, or limiting ideas that need to be dissolved.

You see, the flow not only helps you get where you are *going,* but it also supports you in *growing*—in maturing mentally, emotionally, and spiritually—so you are adequately prepared for where you are headed. It will give you the *time* you need to grow, and it will orchestrate the *opportunities* you need to grow. It may help you meet a particular person who can help you learn a very valuable lesson. Or, it may lead you into a circumstance that will give you some much-needed experience in a certain area.

Some situations you encounter may be quite challenging. But, as I mention in my message titled, "Purposely Choosing Challenges," many of those opportunities for growth are ones that you *yourself*—at very deep level—*know* that you need, and are actually *choosing* to take advantage of, so you can *successfully* live the kind of life that you are pursuing.

So, here's to *rowing* the flow—whether it's fast or slow. And here's to *growing* with the flow—knowing that it is helping you become the kind of person you *need* to be . . . the kind of person you *want* to be . . . and the kind of person you were *born* to be.

39

Divine Confirmation

In my message titled, "Identifying Intuition," I list seven different forms that intuitive guidance can take. Of those seven forms, the one that is the most definitive is the one I call a "Knowing." A Knowing is an inexplicable and unshifting sense of surety. You just Know—with a capital "K"—what your intuitive sense is telling you, and there is absolutely no question about it. You don't need any other evidence to confirm or support the divine guidance that you believe you have received.

However, that experience is relatively rare. Whether you have a dream one night that seems particularly significant, or you experience a coincidence that seems meaningful, in most cases there will still be some *doubt* on your part as to whether you have just received divine guidance, or not. But that's okay! You don't have to instantly know with complete certainty what the Universe is trying to tell you!

What's wonderful about divine guidance is that it doesn't just speak to you in one single way, one single time. When you are truly being guided by The Divine, you will receive *multiple* messages that all point you in the same direction. You may hear the still, small voice of your intuition, and then have it confirmed by an article you see in a magazine, or by something a stranger tells you. You may read something particularly motivational in a book, and then have it supported by the lyrics to a song you hear, or by a sign you see on the side of the highway.

After receiving my message titled, "When The Flow Seems Slow," a woman from Oklahoma (who describes herself as "Ms. Whirlwind USA") wondered whether my message was a "sign" for her to slow down, relax, and just enjoy the still, calm waters that she appeared to be in. Was she, indeed, being divinely encouraged to take it easy for a while? It sure looks that way. Because, within just a few short hours of writing to me about my message, she experienced three synchronistic events that all pointed toward the exact same thing:

> First, she drove by a billboard at a church that read, "It's Summer—A Time To Relax And Spend Time With God."

> Then, a friend called her and asked, "Why do you feel that you always have to be busy? Why not just relax and enjoy the quiet time?"

> Finally, she received an email from her daughter to come over to her house for a night or two and just relax.

Could the message for this woman have been any clearer? I like to call this kind of corroborating evidence "Divine Confirmation." And what a relief it is, because it means that you get more than one chance to receive the message.

Dear reader, do you sense that there is a step that you are being divinely guided to take (or *not* take), but you're not absolutely positive about it yet? Like I said before, that's okay! Just wait! If there is something you are meant to know—*really* meant to know—it will become obvious soon enough. You don't have to "get it" the very first time. You just have to keep paying attention.

40

Dealing With Loss

Since I first began writing these messages in May of 2005, the world has experienced numerous natural disasters, including devastating earthquakes, floods, tsunamis, tornadoes, hurricanes, and wildfires. And there have been numerous manmade tragedies, as well, including some horrific shooting rampages. In the course of these tragic events, countless people have lost their homes, lost their businesses, lost their health, and lost their lives.

I often mention that one of the keys to living life in the divine flow is maintaining a positive attitude. A "merry" mindset is important because it helps you stay open to divine guidance, which enables you to play your part in the unfolding of a greater good. But—and here's the point of this particular message—*that positive attitude must be genuine.* That means that when you experience a loss in your life, feelings such as disappointment, sadness, and sorrow must first be allowed to run their natural course. Only *then* can there be an *authentic* return to a more optimistic outlook on life.

Living life in the divine flow is not—I repeat, *not*—about stuffing your feelings to maintain an "appearance" of positivity. There *is* such a thing as legitimate pain in life. It is not the kind of pain that you bring upon yourself through needless worry, thoughtless actions, or inappropriate attachments. It is the kind of pain that occurs most often with the sudden and unexpected loss of someone you deeply love, or the loss of something else that is near and dear to your heart, such as a fulfilling job or a beloved pet.

If you are dealing with a loss in your life right now—or any challenging situation—it is okay to go ahead and let yourself feel your feelings about it. Give yourself permission to experience all of your feelings freely and fully. Allow them to come, and go . . . and come again . . . and go again. It is the only way that they will eventually dissipate.

If, instead, you attempt to suppress those feelings, they will continue to exist at an unconscious level. And, in the end, that will just delay your ability to heal and feel joy again. And by "joy" I mean that underlying sense of appreciation for the *total* experience of life . . . a joy that embraces *all* of life's twists and turns . . . a joy that might be best described as "bittersweet."

To each of you who have recently lost your home, a loved one, or anything else that occupies an important place in your heart, please know that kindred spirits the world over are supporting you in the restoration of your sense of well-being. And know, too, that even though it may not appear that way right now, with the help of The Divine it is always possible for great good to come out of this time of great grief.

41

The Flow in a Relationship

As I have pointed out before, you rarely—if ever—get anywhere in life completely on your own. Usually, reaching your chosen destinations in life requires the participation, cooperation, and support of others. This is *especially* true when you are in a very close relationship with another person—a spouse, a partner, or a family member, for example.

When your choices immediately and directly affect someone else, it may feel as if you and that other person are literally "in the same boat"—that you are both in the same "Relation Ship," so to speak. That's when rowing your boat in harmony with each other becomes of paramount importance.

The question is, how do you *both* "row with the flow" when the two of you do not immediately agree on a goal, or do not agree on the next right step for reaching a goal? That question is one that I often get asked. And here is my answer:

For a couple to stay in the flow—or even for a close-knit group to move forward in a mutually beneficial way—it is helpful when each person in that relationship is willing to do four things:

1. Take the time to attune himself or herself to his or her inner guidance.

2. Have the patience to wait for that inner guidance to unfold for everyone involved.

3. Practice loving kindness, so each person feels safe enough to express his or her thoughts and feelings.

4. Let go of what he or she originally thought was best.

I have been in a close relationship with my lovely and loving partner, Carol, for many years now. Our daily life together has always felt like it was "in the flow." But does that mean that on a day-to-day basis we *always instantly agree* on every single step we are considering taking? No.

There are plenty of days when we try to point "our boat" in completely different directions. But when that happens, we take the time to slow down and listen to our hearts, as well as listen to each other. We patiently pause, and sense how alternative options "feel." In other words, we focus our attention on our inner guidance system—our intuition.

When we do that, one of two things usually occurs: One of us will let go of his or her plan because it becomes apparent that it was just an ego-driven impulse, and not a true desire of the heart. Or, one of us will be divinely inspired with a *completely new and different idea*—an idea that is mutually beneficial and "feels right" to both of us.

The beauty of intuitive guidance is that it always benefits *all* parties. And why does it? Because the ultimate source of your intuitive guidance is the *One Spirit* that unites us all—that creative, loving, divine energy that we are *all* expressions of . . . resulting in the kind of guidance that is always in the best interests of *everyone*.

So, dear reader, are you in the kind of relationship with another person—or a group of people—where mutual support and cooperation is necessary to get where you want to go? Then remember to treat everyone involved with loving kindness, and take the time to listen to your heart. You will be amazed at how people with diverse needs, ideas, dreams, and desires can all come together and be part of one mutually fulfilling flow . . . an effortless flow . . . a flow that is nothing less than *divine*.

42

Happy Accidents

Have you ever missed a familiar exit on a highway, or passed a street that you fully intended to turn onto, only to discover that your mistake put you on a path to something unexpectedly beneficial? Have you ever made a careless error that immediately resulted in something wonderful happening for you . . . or for others?

You might assume that I am once again writing about the idea that everything can be a stepping-stone to your higher good, if you want it to be. But I'm not. That particular transformational process involves a fair amount of conscious participation on your part, and usually requires a great deal of patience. No, what I am describing here is the type of mistake that has such an *instant* benefit, it seems as if the *mistake itself* was divinely intended.

For instance, in April of 2007 I received an email from a woman who was planning a spiritual conference in Atlanta, Georgia. I was one of her scheduled speakers, and she wanted to go over a few details with me. Well, as it turned out, she had misread the schedule, and she had actually contacted me in error. However, through our correspondence, I discovered that several aspects of my presentation in Atlanta had not been taken care of. So I was able to correct those oversights before I got there. If it weren't for her mistake, I would have had several rude surprises awaiting me when I arrived.

Some people call this particular kind of mistake a "Happy Accident." But no matter what you call it, it's just another way that the divine flow guides us to our good. Here's another example:

A while back, I had some distressing news I needed to deliver to a man I knew named John. Unfortunately, my relationship with John was, to say the least, strained. In fact, contacting him with this piece of information was going to be so awkward, I kept putting it off.

One day, in prayer, I asked God to help me share my message with John in a way that would not only be acceptable to him, but effortless for me. A few days later, a friend of mine named Elaine emailed her new phone number to me. When I looked at her number, I noticed that it was almost exactly the same as John's. In fact, the only difference was that the last two numbers were transposed.

Since Elaine knew John, I decided to call Elaine and let her know about the coincidence. So I dialed her number. And guess who answered? John. I had "accidentally" dialed *John's* number instead of *Elaine's*! As soon as I realized my mistake, I explained my error to John. We then started talking, and—in the end—I was able to deliver the news he needed to know in a very natural and appropriate way. My little mistake had turned out to be a big blessing.

So, was this "happy accident" divinely orchestrated? Did my own inner Spirit actually distract me in some way, causing me to misdial the number? All I can say is that this kind of thing happens to me so often, my answer to both of those questions is a resounding "Yes!"

How about you, dear reader? Have you ever experienced this kind of phenomenon in your life? If not, could it be that you just haven't been fully aware of it? I invite you to start actively watching for happy accidents to occur in your life. I wouldn't be surprised if you experienced a mistake turning into a miracle this very week!

43

Dealing With Uncertainty

E ven when you do your very best to get in touch with your intuitive guidance, and when you earnestly try to pay attention to the divine signs and synchronicities that are leading you forward in life, there will be plenty of days when you will still feel uncertain—confused, even. Should you go this way or that way? Should you do this thing or the other? Often the answer just isn't clear. And as your confusion continues, you may feel increasingly frustrated.

Do you know why confusion is frustrating? Because you believe that you *shouldn't be* confused! Actually, it is only your *resistance* to your state of confusion that is causing you to feel frustrated, and causing you to suffer needlessly. A little confusion is common! It is something that we *all* experience every now and then. But rarely does it persist for any great length of time. Eventually, mixed signals will give way to clear signals, and you will feel comfortable enough to make a choice.

The key to more rapidly reaching that state of divine certainty is to *accept* your confusion when it arises. Instead of hastily and unwisely *forcing* yourself to make a decision, simply acknowledge the fact that—at the moment—you are too unsure to make a decision ... *and be okay with that!*

Remember, to be able to discern your next right step, you must be genuinely open and receptive to divine guidance. And a mind that is in resistance is rarely relaxed enough for that guidance to be readily apparent. In other words, your *resistance* to your confusion is the very thing that may keep you stuck in that uncertain state!

However, that said, what if the time has come when—because of circumstances that are beyond your control or influence—you *have* to make a decision, and yet, you are *still unclear* about how you are being divinely directed. What then? I think you know the answer. When that moment arrives, you simply have to make a decision one way or the other, and then see how things feel ... *afterwards.*

Understandably, waiting to find out if a decision feels right *after the fact* is not desirable. But that situation does not have to be a source of undue stress for you, if you keep in mind one of the fundamental principles for living life in the divine flow. It's the principle I mention the most in these messages: *Everything* can be a stepping-stone to your higher good, if you look at it that way.

Even if you inadvertently make a decision based on the fears of your ego rather than the inspiration of your Spirit, the Universe can *still* guide you to your highest good from *wherever* you wind up. Your job is simply to *remain* open and receptive to divine direction by continuing to maintain a positive outlook.

This process is not unlike what happens when you have a navigation device in your car, but you miss the exit it was directing you to take, or you turn the wrong way. It simply offers you a brand new route from wherever you now happen to be.

Remember, too, that there are always valuable lessons to be learned from whatever circumstance you find yourself in. That means that every decision you make—divinely inspired or not—gives you an opportunity to gain further clarity about yourself, and to grow in wisdom, compassion, understanding, and so on. I know one woman, for example, who started a brand new job and knew *immediately* that it wasn't a very good fit for her. As a result of that experience, however, she became much clearer about what kind of career path she *did* want to pursue. And the Universe quickly helped her move in that direction.

So, dear reader, *before* you take any step, do your best to discern whether that step *truly is* your next right step, or not. But if you are still not completely sure, don't worry too much about that. Living life in the divine flow is not about being 100% certain, 100% of the time. It's about making the best choice you can with the information and experience you currently have, knowing that—no matter what decision you finally make—the Universe can always "make it right" in the end.

44

The Process of Manifesting

D o you think you would be happier if you could *instantly*
manifest whatever it is you want to have, do, or be in
your life? Would you happier if you could just snap your
fingers and *immediately* a brand new car would appear in
your garage, or *suddenly* you would find yourself in a brand
new job? Believe it or not, I don't think you would find that
kind of instantaneous manifestation very satisfying—at least,
not on an ongoing basis.

Like I state in my message titled, "Motherhood and
Manifesting," you will always be conceiving of things you
want to have, do, or be in life. And you will always be going
about the business of manifesting those ideas in the material
world. But that process is . . . well . . . *a process!* And the *real
joy* of manifesting—of creating—lies *in the process itself.*

Take a painter, for example. Is a painter happy when he
or she has finished an original work of art? Of course. But the
real enjoyment of painting came with each and every stroke
of the brush. It was the experience of *painting*—not just
having painted—that was fulfilling. Do you think a painter

would continue to paint if every time he or she visualized a picture it just somehow magically appeared on the canvas? I don't think so.

Like a painter creating a work of art one stroke of the brush at a time, you manifest what you want in life one stroke of your "oars" at a time. Don't make the mistake of putting off your happiness until you actually *reach* your chosen "destination"—until you actually accomplish your goal, fulfill your desire, or realize your dream.

Whether you are building a home, raising a family, or launching a career, consciously choose to savor each and every moment of the journey. Because that, dear reader, is where the real satisfaction lies.

45

Does Negativity Have Power?

C ountless books and articles have been written about a principle called the "Law of Attraction," and the power we seem to have to "attract" into our lives whatever it is we focus our attention on. The authors of those books and articles usually caution us to avoid negative thinking, and warn us to avoid dwelling on that which we do not want . . . and for a very good reason. It is commonly believed that negative thoughts have just as much power as positive thoughts. So, if we continually focus on negative outcomes instead of positive ones, then *that* is what we will attract into our lives . . . even though those outcomes are not something that we desire.

I don't dispute the fact that undesirable outcomes *can* manifest when we continually harbor negative thoughts. But I *do wonder* if negativity has the power to attract something into our lives in the exact same way positivity does. The reason I question that belief is for one simple reason. It just doesn't fit my own experience of life.

You see, for many, many years I was a very negative person—constantly fearful and worried, and always expecting the worst to happen. Occasionally, yes, my fears would come true to one extent or another. More often than not, though, something *good* would happen instead. Even when I acted in ways that were obviously self-destructive, I was often miraculously saved from any real harm.

So, as I began to read more and more about the Law of Attraction, I began to wonder about a few things, such as:

> Why doesn't my chronic negativity *always* have the negative effects it should have according to the Law of Attraction?

> Why—in spite of my many negative thoughts and feelings—do *good* things often happen instead?

> Why, in my experience, does negativity seem much *weaker* than positivity? Is it a *lesser* power?

Through a process of observation, contemplation, meditation, and what I consider to be nothing less than divine inspiration, this—in part—is the conclusion I reached:

> *Negativity is not the power to create negatively.*
> *It is simply a self-induced reduction*
> *in the power to create positively.*

Allow me to explain: I believe that there is tremendous power in positivity. When you think positive thoughts, feel positive feelings, and foster positive and loving intentions, you do—*literally*—attract into your life the people and circumstances that lead you to the effortless fulfillment of your heart's desires.

What's more, it is relatively easy for you to recognize and cooperate with what you are attracting into your life, because positivity keeps you open and receptive to G.O.D.—the Guidance Of the Divine. You are more insightful, more inspired, and more intuitive . . . and you make much *wiser* choices as a result.

When you consistently entertain negative thoughts, you experience something quite different. Surprisingly, even when you are in a *negative* state of mind, you *still* attract into your life the people and circumstances that can be highly beneficial to you. Why? Because this intelligent Universe of ours knows what lies *beneath* your negativity. It knows what you *really* want. It knows what you *really* need. And, because of its beneficent nature, it continues to work on your behalf to help you manifest those desires, in spite of your negative mindset!

However—and here's the crux of this message—*negativity makes it extremely difficult for you to recognize and cooperate with what the Universe is orchestrating for you!*

Like I mention in my message that is titled, "Imaginary Troubles," when you harbor negative thoughts and feelings, you severely restrict your ability to be open and receptive to divine guidance. It is harder to see what the divine signs are trying to show you. It is harder to hear what your intuition is trying to tell you. And thus, you are much more likely to make *unwise* choices—choices based solely on your own limited knowledge and biased perceptions.

When doubt and dread rule your head, you are *bound* to have some undesirable experiences in life. But it is not because you literally "attracted" those experiences to you through some kind of magnetic power. For the most part, those experiences are simply the *natural consequence* of going through life without the advantage of divine direction—of moving through life unguided or misguided. As I illustrate this concept in *Row, Row, Row Your Boat:*

> "It's like trying to make your way across an unfamiliar room in the middle of the night. Without a guiding light, it's almost impossible to avoid bumping into something. But you did not *attract* that something to you. You simply ran into it because you couldn't see it in the darkness. You did not *attract* a collision. You were simply more susceptible to a collision as the natural result of your blindness."

Dear reader, are you stumbling around in the night, blindly bumping into things you don't want or like? Do you want to regain your power to create what you *do* want in life? Then turn on the light! It's the light that illuminates your path by illuminating your mind. It's the Light of the Divine that resides deep within your own heart. And all it takes for you to turn on that helpful, guiding light is just a little bit of positivity.

46

Don't Believe Everything
You Think!

The other day I was driving down the road when I saw a
bumper sticker on the car in front of me that read . . .

DON'T BELIEVE EVERYTHING YOU THINK!

I love that bumper sticker, because it perfectly captures the
essence of one of the most important principles for living life
in the divine flow: You must let go of what you "think" you
know.

One of the ways that you may be inadvertently
interfering with the flow is by thinking that you know best,
and overruling the divine guidance that you are continually
receiving through various sources—such as your own intuitive
sense. I'm certainly not suggesting here that you *forget*
everything you think you know. I'm just reminding you of the
obvious truth that there is always *more to know* than you
currently know. And when you keep an open mind to new
and different information—even when it conflicts with your
current understanding—your ability to receive divine direction

will be greatly enhanced.

Remember, too, that most of your thoughts are either reflections on the *past* or projections into the *future*. And since divine guidance always comes to you in the *present*, the very act of thinking can limit your ability to be in the flow.

The phrase, "being lost in thought," is very appropriate in this case, because whenever you are not consciously in the "now," you are much more likely to *miss* the divine signposts that can show you the best way to get where you're going. You become unguided or misguided by your lack of present moment awareness, and thus, *lost*!

Even the *way* you think can limit your experience of the flow. When you are fearful, for instance, you may connect one thought to another so quickly, you create a block that prevents divinely inspired ideas from entering your consciousness.

The phrase, "a train of thought," comes to mind here, because that is exactly what a lot of fear-based thinking resembles—a train . . . one car closely coupled to another, and to another, and to another. And often, that train of thought gains so much momentum as it moves along, it is extremely difficult to slow it down, change tracks, and move in a more beneficial direction.

That is why I recommend a daily practice of meditation. Meditation not only slows down your thinking, it helps open up "gaps" between your thoughts, so it is easier for divine insights and intuitive guidance to get through.

So, do you want to live life in the divine flow? You do? Then I suggest you heed the following three suggestions, which I will express here, appropriately enough, as "bumper stickers:"

DON'T BELIEVE EVERYTHING
YOU THINK!

DON'T GET LOST IN THOUGHT!

And finally,

BEFORE THAT TRAIN OF THOUGHT
GOES TOO FAR . . . GET OFF!

47

Fatherhood and The Flow

Many of the churches where I present my talks and workshops refer to the Divine Power at work in this world as "Father-Mother-God." The reason is apparent. It is a simple reminder that this Higher Power that many of us call God, not only has a nature that we associate with fatherhood, but it also has characteristics that we associate with motherhood . . . such as nurturing.

I've never had an issue with the notion of God as *Mother*. But I'll be perfectly honest with you. For much of my life I was very uncomfortable with the concept of God as *Father*. You see, I used to harbor a lot of resentments towards my own father, and whenever I heard the word "Father" used in reference to God, I would cringe a little.

Then one day I had a revelation—one so simple, I was astounded that it didn't occur to me sooner. I remembered that *I was a father*. And what, as a father, did I feel towards my children? Nothing but unconditional love. And what, as a father, did I want for my children? Nothing but for them to be happy and fulfilled, and I would gladly do anything in my power to help them live abundant and joyful lives.

For the first time, I could finally relate to idea of God as *Father*—as a loving, generous, powerful presence in my life that was continually providing for my needs, and continually guiding me towards the fulfillment of my heart's desires.

At that moment, I not only changed the way I felt about *God* as Father, but I began to feel differently about *my own* father, as well. I began to look beyond his human shortcomings to see the divinely loving Spirit within him. And I am happy to say that today I can truly appreciate many things about my father that I ignored or took for granted in the past.

Here's to all the men who have been "fathers" in our lives—who have provided for our well-being, and guided us in effective ways of providing for ourselves . . . just like the divine flow guides and provides. Here's to our earthly fathers, and here's to our heavenly one, as well.

48

You Are Worthy!

In 2008, and again in 2011, I attended the christenings of my first two grandsons, Cole Westmoreland Thomas and Tanner Taylor Thomas. Regardless of what christening may literally mean in various religious circles, I like to think of christening as a ceremony in which the true identity of a baby is named and proclaimed. And what is that true identity? It is the same identity that you, and I, and everyone on this planet share: We are all Children of The Divine—individual expressions of that loving and creative energy we call God.

As Children of The Divine we are all divinely loved, divinely protected, and divinely entitled to lives of peace, prosperity, and fulfillment. And to enjoy these divine privileges we don't have to do a single thing. Just the fact that we exist—just *being*—is reason enough for these heavenly blessings to be bestowed upon us.

Unfortunately, we don't always *feel* this sense of divine entitlement, do we? Instead of feeling that we have a divine right to whatever it is we want to have, do, or be in life, we may feel that we don't deserve to have our dreams come true.

We may feel that we are not good enough, or smart enough, or capable enough. In a word, we may feel that we are not "worthy."

This is a big issue, because our thoughts about ourselves influence the choices that we make in life. And choices based on feelings of low self-worth can easily sabotage our ability to fulfill our heart's desires.

I wish there was a magic wand I could wave that would cause every single person on this planet to immediately recognize his or her innate worth as a beloved Child of The Divine. Obviously, I don't have a wand like that. However, I do have a helpful tool. It's an Affirmation of Worth that "wrote itself" through me a number of years ago. If you are struggling with your sense of worthiness, I hope you find this Affirmation to be helpful.

AN AFFIRMATION OF WORTH

God is All That Is.
And I am part of All That Is.
I now acknowledge my innate worth
as a vital part of The Divine Whole.

It is through me that God knows God's Self
in a way that no other experience can duplicate.

God cherishes my existence,
and it is God's great pleasure
to help me fulfill my heart's desires effortlessly.

It doesn't matter to whom I was born,
or what circumstances followed.
Nor does it matter
how anyone else perceives my value.

I know that I am a precious and essential
part of this Universe . . .
that I have a right to be here,
and that I have a special purpose to fulfill
in this time and place.

I am wanted.
I am needed.
I am worthy and deserving.

I am a Holy Child of The Divine.
Peace, joy, and prosperity
are mine by divine right.
And I claim my divine inheritance now!

49

Constant Surrender

A while back, a dear friend of mine named Judi experienced one of those days when "everything that *can* go wrong, *did* go wrong." Judi was in charge of a Potluck Lunch to be held at her church—an event that was usually attended by about 70 people. That day, the electricity went out, so any food that required heating had to be eaten cold, or not served at all. It was a particularly hot, humid afternoon, and without electricity there was no air conditioning. And when they tried to open the windows for some relief, only one would budge, so they couldn't even catch a breeze. Then, to make matters worse, the toilets overflowed.

After noticing how smoothly and calmly Judi continually adjusted to the ever-worsening situation, a woman came up to her and said, "Wow, Judi, you sure know how to go with the flow!" When Judi got home that evening, she immediately called me to express her appreciation for teaching her how to be—and stay—in the flow. As we spoke, though, it occurred to me that her gratitude was perhaps unnecessary.

Even without the benefit of my teachings, there is a

very good possibility that Judi would have been in the flow anyway. How so? Simply because it is *easier* to be in the flow when things *really* get out of hand, than it is when things are just *slightly* unmanageable. It is when things are *obviously* out of control that we more readily relinquish the idea that we *can* control what is going on, and we tend to surrender.

It is in that state of surrender that we become *genuinely* open to whatever is required of us in that moment. We stop resisting what is, and we stop trying to force things to go the way we "think" they should go. Instead, we desire only to know the next right step that will be in the best interests of all. And it is in that state of genuine receptivity that we begin hear and heed the still, small voice of Spirit that is always there to guide us forward.

The *real* challenge—which is what I am building up to here—is giving up personal control when the situation *does* seem controllable. You see, living life in the divine flow requires you to *constantly* stay in "surrender mode"—no matter how easy it would be for you to manipulate a situation to your liking.

That doesn't mean that you never take any action. It just means that *before* you take any action, you get quiet, go within, and try to get in touch with the wisdom of your Spirit. You might be inspired to take some kind of action that you have never taken before. Or, you may be guided to *refrain* from taking any action at that particular moment. The goal is just to avoid jumping to conclusions and acting hastily.

Remember that living life in the divine flow is about being willing to seek divine guidance in *every* situation—

even the situations that look like you can easily and instantly handle them "on your own." That kind of mindfulness will require a conscious effort on your part, true. And it may require a fair amount of humility, too. But believe me, the outcome will be well worth it.

50

A Charmed Life

Several months ago, Carol and I entertained a couple from Dallas, Texas who had come to our beautiful town of Sedona, Arizona for a short vacation. We took them on one of our favorite hikes—a hike that leads to a small plateau that has some natural caves near the top.

As we relaxed at the mouth of one of those caves, we began to discuss our various philosophies of life. Although Carol and I had known the gentleman for many years, we didn't know his fiancé very well, and she was unfamiliar with my particular focus in life. When I described some of the miracles in my life that have led me to believe in what I call "The Divine Flow," she replied, "Wow, Steven, you have certainly lived a charmed life."

Charmed life? It was at that point I realized that she didn't fully grasp what I way trying to communicate to her. Being *charmed* has little to do with the goodness I have experienced in my life. Nor does *luck* or *good fortune.* I have found that—for the most part—a charmed life is something that you can *consciously create* whenever you practice the principles for living life in the divine flow. A charmed life is what occurs naturally whenever you:

- Pay attention to your intuition

- Notice signs and synchronicities and try to discern their meaning

- Let go of your preconceived ideas and plans

- Release your attachment to specific outcomes

- See everything that happens as a stepping-stone to your highest good

- Treat others, and yourself, with loving kindness

In other words, a charmed life is the natural result of being attentive, flexible, positive, and loving. Here is a nice little example of what can happen when you practice just a couple of those principles:

Two dear friends of mine, Gary and Suzanne, were planning to go to an evening concert to which they already had tickets. As the afternoon progressed, they found themselves running very, very late, with absolutely no hope of getting to the concert on time.

Two actions immediately came to mind: They could give up and not go to the concert at all, knowing that it was the policy of the concert hall to re-sell seats that were not occupied by show time. Or, they could drive like crazy to get there as fast as possible, and risk getting a traffic ticket or having an accident.

On further reflection, however, Gary and Suzanne both had a "feeling" that the *best* course of action would be to simply go ahead and drive to the concert hall at a normal rate of speed, and be completely open and receptive to whatever occurred. In other words, they decided to follow their intuition and remain flexible. And guess what? As a result of that decision, they experienced good fortune in three different ways:

> First, they were so late getting to the concert hall, the parking attendants were no longer collecting the $5 parking fee. So they saved a little money.

> Second, they were so late getting there, some of the staff had already gone home, opening up a perfect parking spot.

> And third, even though their seats had, indeed, been sold to someone else, they were offered two much better seats—seats in the center section, right up front.

Yes, Gary and Suzanne did miss part of the opening number. But all of those nice little extras more than made up for that. You may be tempted to say that Gary and Suzanne were just plain lucky. But I believe their good fortune was the direct result of their decision to consult their inner guidance and do what "felt right"—even though they weren't sure how things would turn out.

So, dear reader, do you want to live a charmed life? Do you want to enjoy a life of ease, grace, and incredible good fortune? Then consistently take the six actions listed at the beginning of this message. Do those things, and you, too, can live a life that some would say is "just plain lucky" . . . a life that *I* would say is being lived "in the flow."

51

Freedom and The Flow

H ere in the United States, July 4th is Independence Day, the day we celebrate our right as a people to create our own futures and pursue our own dreams, free from oppressive and dictatorial rule.

But let us remember, too, that when it comes to our relationship with that Divine Intelligence that we commonly call God, *every* day is Independence Day, and should be recognized and celebrated as such. Each and every day, you have the freedom—the independence—to choose what you want to have in life, what you want to do in life, and what you want to be in life. And you have the freedom to pursue those goals in any way that you see fit.

That doesn't mean that accomplishing those goals is totally up to you, and you alone. Quite the contrary. You are continually receiving *divine* assistance. You are constantly being *divinely guided* and *divinely supported* in fulfilling your heart's desires in the most beneficial way possible. But you will never—ever—be *forced* to do anything that you don't *choose* to do.

You always have the freedom to follow divine guidance, or not. You can choose to row *with* the divine flow, and reach your chosen destinations with effortless ease. Or, you can choose to take a more arduous route, and row *against* the flow by ignoring or resisting divine direction. It's up to you.

The wonderful thing about your freedom of choice is this: Every choice you make in life—whether it is divinely guided or unguided, divinely inspired or ego-driven—gives you an opportunity to learn from your experience, to grow in wisdom and compassion, and to ultimately discover more about your own divinely loving and creative nature. But again, it's your choice. You can choose to learn and grow from the experiences you create . . . or not.

Here's to the joy that comes from creating our lives and living our lives *by choice*. May we always be grateful for the freedom we have to do that.

52

Divine Discontent

Have you ever heard of something called "Divine Discontent?" Divine discontent is not the kind of discontent that arises from your ego. Your ego is *always* discontented—*always* urging you to look outside of yourself for something else or something more to "make you happy." When you experience *divine* discontent, you are not looking for anything outside of yourself to make you happy. You know that true happiness always comes from within. And yet, you *still* have a strange and persistent feeling that something needs to shift in your life.

Sometimes, this feeling arises after you have successfully reached a chosen destination in life. And that's not at all surprising, because on the level of your innately creative Spirit, true satisfaction in life arises from the *process* of manifesting. Once something has been manifested, your Spirit is hungry to create anew, and it inspires you to begin the process all over again. That's why a painter doesn't stop painting after completing a single work of art—even if it's considered to be a masterpiece. He or she will continue to create one work of art after another.

Sometimes, too, this feeling of divine discontent is a signal from your Spirit that you are ready to move into an even more fulfilling phase of your work life. Even though you may be very accomplished at what you do, well suited to it, and handsomely paid for it, part of you may long to use your talents, skills, and abilities in an even more meaningful and worthwhile way.

Dear reader, are you feeling discontented right now? Through prayer, meditation, and/or contemplation, see if you can discern the *true* source of that feeling. Are you actually just being critical and judgmental about your life? Or, are you truly *grateful* for what you have in life, but you *still* sense that there is something else you should be doing.

Perhaps it is time to seriously consider what brings you the most joy and satisfaction in life—regardless of the income you think it may or may not generate—and begin devoting more time and energy to that. Perhaps you are being encouraged by your Spirit to recognize your "calling," and to finally step out in faith and follow that call. Perhaps it is time to heed that subtle stirring from deep within that says, "It's time for a new chapter in your life to begin." Just something to ponder.

53

Your Calling and The Flow

When I was inspired to write and publish my first book, I experienced the divine flow in my life like never before. With incredible ease and grace, I was unmistakably directed to the publisher of my book; the cover photo was divinely delivered to me; three of the notable people who first endorsed my book literally showed up on the doorstep of my church; and my first significant speaking engagement was a rare opportunity that just "came my way." Even while I was writing my book, I received some unexpected income to help support me during that lengthy process.

The reason, I believe, that the flow was so consistent and so obvious in this instance, was simply because the activity that I was engaged in was directly related to my "calling." A calling is something that you are extremely passionate about. It is something that adds purpose and meaning to your life. It is something that you have an inborn talent for, find extremely fulfilling, and would do even if you received no income for doing it.

I found my calling when I was first invited to teach a

weekly class for a group of adults at a Unity church in Dallas, Texas. I had never done anything even remotely like that before. But I found it to be the single most fulfilling experience of my life. Within a very short amount of time I knew that I had found my life's purpose. I knew that I was on this earth to use my skills and abilities as a communicator to deliver a message. And that message was that we live in an incredibly beneficent Universe—a Universe that is continually working on our behalf to help us fulfill our heart's desires.

So why—once I found my calling—would I have noticed the flow to such an elevated degree? It is simply because a calling is a true desire of the heart. And being consciously aware of that calling meant that my *head* was aligned with my *heart,* and that *every* part of me was open and receptive to moving in the same direction.

One of the main obstacles to living life in the divine flow is that your heart may be encouraging you to go in one direction, while your head is looking in another direction. That makes it extremely difficult for you to see the divine signs that are pointing you toward your highest good, and toward your greatest joy.

Have you found your calling yet? If not, begin by asking yourself a few simple questions. What are you good at? What unique combination of talents, skills, or abilities do you have? What brings you the most joy? What have you been fascinated with your whole life?

Keep in mind that your calling is not always the same thing as your job or your career. It may simply be a special gift that you have to share with this world, while—at the same time—you are engaged in other activities to generate an income. Perhaps your calling is to bring more harmony into the world as a peacemaker. Perhaps it is to bring more wholeness into the world as a healer. Or perhaps it is to bring more understanding into the world as a spiritual guide.

Here's to finding your passion in life . . . your purpose . . . your calling. And more than that, here's to answering that call. When you do, I guarantee you this: It will feel as if the entire Universe is bending over backwards to support you in your endeavor. Because it is!

54

Our Shared Mission

In my last message—the one titled, "Your Calling and The Flow"—I described what a "calling" is, and I explained why you will experience the divine flow in a heightened way when you are actively engaged in that calling. A calling, as I pointed out, is something that you are so passionate about, you would do it even if you were not paid for it.

That makes a calling different from a job, because—strictly speaking—a job is something you do solely for the income it provides. A calling is different from a career, too, because—again, strictly speaking—a career is also something you do for the income it provides, but it happens to be something that you are very interested in, and you are perfectly content doing that same thing for years on end.

The point of this message is this: In the big picture, it really doesn't make any difference *what* you are engaged in—a job, a career, or a calling—*as long as you are doing it with love.*

You see, although we may have different callings in life, and we may spend our days engaged in very different occupations, there is one thing that we all have in common. And that is our underlying mission. It is a "Mission from God," so to speak. And what exactly *is* that shared mission? It is simply the mission to discover, express, and experience the Truth of who we really are at the core of our being—the divine essence of love itself.

To paraphrase Marianne Williamson, from her classic book, *A Return to Love*: Knowing who you are and why you really came here is more important than knowing what you want to do. What you want to do is not the important question. The question to ask is, "When I do *anything*, how should I do it?'" And the answer is, "With loving kindness."

Whether you spend your day in front of a computer, behind the counter of a retail store, under a car at an automotive repair shop, or you oversee the work of dozens of people at a large corporation, always remember to be love, spread love, and let love lead the way. That, dear reader, is the real key to living life in the divine flow . . . and it is the key to living a life that is full of joy and meaning.

55

The Flow of Abundance

By simply observing nature, we can learn a lot about living life in the divine flow. For example, the way a tree bends in the wind reminds us of the importance of being flexible instead of rigid. And the way a flower pops up from a crack in the concrete reminds us that a blessing can bloom in almost any environment.

And then there is the way one hummingbird will tenaciously guard a feeder and scare away all the other hummingbirds that come to eat, which reminds us that we live in a world of lack and limitation, and there is simply not enough good to go around. What? Well, that's certainly how it appears when you watch the way some hummingbirds behave. "There is not enough! This is mine!" That seems to be the general idea that some of these tiny birds are expressing. Sound familiar? Know any human beings with that kind of mind-set?

Obviously, dear reader, the lesson here is *not* that the Universe is limited in its ability to amply supply everyone's needs. The lesson here is quite the opposite.

I believe we live in an *infinitely abundant* Universe—a Universe that is continually responding to everyone's needs through an *unlimited number of channels*. We block our experience of that abundant flow, however, whenever we remain too narrowly focused on the channels of abundance that we are already familiar with, such as our employers, our benefactors, or the government. The fact is, the Universe is *infinitely inventive* in coming up with ways to prosper us.

I once read about a man who bit into a clam in a Florida restaurant and discovered a purple pearl worth $25,000. Not only are purple pearls extremely rare, but it is also very unusual to find a pearl inside of a clam instead of an oyster. And clams are not even something that this gentleman typically orders!

And then there was the time that I needed an additional $2,500 to pay some unexpected bills. One day, my car was slightly damaged in a shower of cement fragments that fell from an office building that I was parked next to. The damage was very minor—just a few nicks and dings here and there. But because the damage was spread across several panels of the car, the cost of repairs was much more than one would expect. The owner of the building, though, was happy to write me a check for that expense—a check that I used to pay my bills instead of repair the car . . . a check for exactly $2,500.

Like I said earlier, the Universe is *infinitely inventive* in coming up with ways to prosper us. Our challenge is to remain open and receptive to *any and all* channels of prosperity—even the most unlikely ones. And that means we must be open and receptive to following divine guidance, *even when we don't understand where it is leading us.*

It is important, too, to keep in mind that a *channel* of prosperity is not the same thing as the *source* of our prosperity. The *ultimate origin* of our abundance is that Infinite and Eternal Field of Supply that *lies behind* every channel. When we start to think of any one channel as being our source, there is always an underlying fear that this source may one day go away. And that fear interferes with our ability to stay attuned to the divine flow, and do what we are being divinely directed to do in the moment.

Through our faith in an unending source of supply, may we overcome our fear, so we can more readily hear that still, small voice that is suggesting our next right step—a step that may be as simple as "order the clams," or "park here." And, with all due respect to certain hummingbirds, may our mind-set continually be this one: "There is more than enough for everyone! So let's all share!"

56

The Extraordinary
in the Ordinary

In my preceding message titled, "The Flow of Abundance," I wrote about the true source of prosperity, and how the divine flow can prosper you in ways that are—to say the least—surprising. That doesn't mean, of course, that abundance can't also flow to you through channels that you expect. Often you may experience prosperity in a completely predictable manner. But even in those ordinary circumstances, you can still sense the divine flow at work. Here's a nice example:

When Carol and I moved to Sedona, Carol found work as a part-time innkeeper at a beautiful Bed & Breakfast Lodge in the center of town. Although she was happy in her work, a full-time position with benefits would have been preferable.

Well, after two years of service, Carol's hours—which already weren't enough—were practically cut in half. This was due to the sudden and dramatic economic downturn the country experienced at that time. At that moment, Carol got a very strong feeling that it was time for her to move on, and she began to affirm for a better position—one that would not only offer her a full-time salary with benefits, but also a regular schedule, a harmonious environment, and work that was perfectly suited to her talents and interests.

Lo and behold, the very first time she looked in the Help Wanted section of the local newspaper, there it was: an ad for an organization that needed an administrative assistant to replace someone who was retiring. It was a full-time position, with regular hours, plus benefits. And, as it turned out, Carol was uniquely qualified for the job.

You see, there was one requirement for this job that was out of the ordinary. The particular organization that was running this ad was a Metaphysical University, and every applicant was required to have a background in metaphysical studies—the kind of principles that are taught in New Thought churches such as Unity and Religious Science. Carol has been a New Thought student since the age of eight!

Carol quickly emailed her resume to the school, and they called her the very next day to set up an interview. When she arrived for the interview, she was surprised to discover that the person she would be replacing is someone she already knew from the Unity Church of Sedona. This lovely lady had noticed Carol's resume among the others, and had already encouraged the founder of the university to interview her for the position.

When Carol returned home from the interview she was beaming with joy. Not only had the interview gone well, but she absolutely loved the spiritually oriented environment in which she might be working. To Carol, it felt like a match made in Heaven. And it must have been just that, because two days later Carol was offered the job!

Now, on the surface, this story may seem somewhat unremarkable: Carol wanted a new job. She looked in the paper. She found one that looked good. She interviewed for the job. And she happened to get it. But when you consider the *synchronicity* of the timing, the *coincidence* of the particular person who was retiring, and the *perfect match* to Carol's talents, interests, and background, it is easy to see the divine flow at work.

Dear reader, do you have a particular desire that you are pursuing right now? Then make sure that you don't miss your miracle by ignoring some of the more traditional paths that may lead to the fulfillment of that desire. Be open to the extraordinary in the ordinary. When you are consistently graced with effortless ease, and you are constantly blessed by feelings of peace and joy, you can be certain that the path you are on is no accident . . . but one that has been divinely orchestrated for your highest good.

57

The Divine Appointment
in Disappointment

In my last message—the one titled, "The Extraordinary in the Ordinary"—I wrote about Carol's effortless manifestation of a wonderful new job, in a time when many people were having the *opposite* experience. Naturally, Carol was elated to secure her new position so easily. But here's what I didn't mention in that message: If Carol had *not* been hired—if someone *else* had been chosen instead—Carol would have been perfectly at peace with that.

That's not to say that Carol wouldn't have been momentarily disappointed. But she would have seen the "divine appointment" in her disappointment. Said another way, Carol would have assumed that *not* getting that particular job was a *good* thing, because there must be something even *better* waiting for her—a perfect position that she was still being guided to. And there is a good reason why Carol would have believed that to be true.

You see, Carol did an absolutely marvelous job of staying in the divine flow during her job-hunting process. Here is what she did:

- She began with a clear intention of what kind of work experience she wanted to have.

- She stayed awake and aware in the now moment, watching for the divine flow to present the next right step to her.

- She took each right step as it came along— without hesitation.

- She continually monitored her feelings, and made decisions based on a sense of peace and ease, rather than fear.

- She never forced something to go the way she "thought" it should go.

- She let go of any rigid attachment to a particular outcome.

One single step at a time, Carol was *willing* to allow the divine flow to guide her to her *highest* good—which *could* be the job that she saw advertised in the newspaper . . . *or* its equivalent . . . *or* something even greater.

The point, dear reader, is this: When you follow Carol's example—when you *consciously* pay attention to what's going on within you and around you, and when you are *truly willing* to let go of what you "think" you know, and focus only on the step that is right in front of you—*everything* that occurs will feel divinely orchestrated and "meant to be." Even if something happens that disappoints you, that feeling will quickly be replaced by a sense that you are closer than ever to your highest good.

Here's to living life in the divine flow, and experiencing that peaceful, happy feeling that comes from knowing that you are still being guided to a divine appointment, even when you are faced with disappointment.

58

The Illusion of Control

On the page of my website called, "About The Author," there is a sentence that says that I am a "recovering control-freak." Notice the word *recovering*. It doesn't say *recovered*.

Yes, even though I am one of the world's foremost masters at living life in the divine flow (a great big smile and a wink go here), when something happens that "threatens" me, I am still occasionally challenged by the urge to make a decision or take an action for the *sole purpose* of making me feel secure again.

I am not talking here about *divinely guided* decisions or *divinely directed* actions. I am talking about choices that fool me into feeling like I am in the "driver's seat" again—that I am in control of the situation, and thus, in control of my future. But am I ever really in control? Are any of us ever really in control of anything?

The answer is, of course, no. *Control is merely an illusion.* No matter how well we have organized our lives, and no matter much we think we have all of our "ducks in a row," life can—and frequently does—surprise us.

Now, that doesn't mean that you should never make any plans. You might be surprised to know that I am actually a very big planner. But—and this is what's key—I am willing to *alter* or *let go* of my plans quickly, because I recognize that the course of life can change in the blink of an eye. Planning is not a problem in and of itself. Remaining *rigidly attached* to a plan is the problem.

To live life in the divine flow is to accept the *uncertainty* of life, and find your security in the knowledge that no matter what happens—or why—the divine flow continues to guide you to your highest good from *right where you are, wherever you are.*

Living life in the divine flow is *not* about taking a step in order to feel secure again. It is about taking a step that arises out of the security that you *already* feel—the security that comes from knowing that you are always divinely protected, because you are always being divinely directed. Your job is to be patient enough, prayerful enough, introspective enough, and observant enough to discern that divine direction in the midst of changing, surprising, or unwanted circumstances.

May you, me, and *all* of us aspire to become true "Masters of The Flow" . . . rather than "Masters of Illusion."

59

The Bigger Picture

When Carol and I moved to Sedona, we quickly noticed an interesting phenomenon in the first house we rented. There is a large picture window in the living room of that house that perfectly frames one of the most popular sights in Sedona—a Red Rock formation called Bell Rock. When viewed from the living room, Bell Rock fills much of the window, and it looks huge. But when you step outside onto the patio, Bell Rock seems to dramatically shrink.

Why is that? It's because when you are outside you see the *whole* picture. You see the vast blue sky above Bell Rock, all of the terrain beneath it, and the mountains that flank Bell Rock on both the left and the right. In that context, Bell Rock appears to be relatively small.

Isn't life like that? Mountains often represent the challenges you face in life; and, yes, some challenges can be quite significant. But when they are viewed through the confines of your limited perception—when they are "framed" by your highly personal, highly biased, and highly subjective beliefs and fears—those challenges can seem much larger than they actually are.

When, instead, you look at the *bigger picture,* and let go of how you are *framing* the object of your attention, challenges become less insurmountable and more manageable. And what, exactly, *is* the bigger picture?

Well, for one, it helps to remember that you never have to overcome any troubling circumstance completely on your own. You have the *whole Universe* on your side—a Universe that is continually working on your behalf to help you solve any particular problem that you might have. And to the Universe—to that intelligent, compassionate energy that we call God—*every* problem, regardless of its seeming size and complexity, is eminently solvable.

Secondly, it helps to keep in mind that any current challenge that you are facing is just one small *portion* of your *entire* life experience. Yes, that portion may be totally dominating your experience at the moment—in fact, it may be all that you are able to focus on right now—but eventually you will come to see that situation as just *one part* of the *complete* picture of your life.

Remember that no matter how enormous your current difficulty appears to be, it really only looks that way from your restricted point of view. The Truth is, *all* challenges are *smaller* challenges when viewed in the context of God's unlimited love, and God's infinite inventiveness. *All* problems are *smaller* problems when you are able to look at the bigger picture. I hope you find as much comfort in that thought as I do.

60

A Step Already Taken?

Since 2004, I have been the guest speaker at more than ninety churches in sixteen states. I have been invited to speak at five national conferences. And I have shared my message with dozens of other organizations, as well. On more than once occasion, an appreciative person has asked me if I received some kind of formal training in public speaking. The answer is no. However, fairly early in life I was encouraged to be in some amateur theater productions, which helped me get over my painfully shy nature at the time. In my career as an advertising writer, I was frequently required to present my ideas to small groups of people. And later in life, I was asked to teach an adult class at my church, which I happily did week after week for eight years.

The result of those experiences was this: Once I determined that my next right step as a spiritual author was to promote my book and its message by speaking to as many congregations and organizations as possible, that step was a virtually effortless one for me to take.

Does that mean that all of those prior experiences were

divinely orchestrated to make it easier for me to be a good public speaker? That is certainly possible. All I know for sure is this: Sometimes you are *already* taking your next right step, and you don't even realize it. Once in a while there are activities that you engage in—either by choice or by necessity—that turn out to be very helpful steps in the unfolding of your good. Here's another example:

After publishing *Row, Row, Row Your Boat,* it was my intention to write a follow-up book. But I never felt like I had the time to sit down and do it. One day, a friend of mine asked me to email her with regular notices about my ever-changing speaking schedule. That same week, two more people requested the very same thing. Sensing that this was the divine flow, I began to honor those requests. But I didn't just send out a schedule. I decided to add an inspirational thought along with it. And thus, my weekly inspirational messages were born.

I had been sending out these messages for about six months, when someone asked me if I was going to write a second book. As usual, I replied that I *intended* to write a second book, but I just didn't have the time to sit down and do it. And then this person said to me, "Couldn't your weekly messages be your second book?"

At that moment I realized two things: Not only *could* my messages be my second book, they *would* be my second book! And better yet, *it was already partially written!* I was *already* taking the step I needed to take to fulfill my desire, and I didn't even know it. And now, you are reading the result of that step already taken.

Dear reader, what I would like for you to take away from these two examples is this: If you are feeling divinely inspired to take a certain action, but it doesn't seem to have anything to do with accomplishing a particular goal that you currently have in mind . . . *do it anyway!* You never know what it may lead to, what it may prepare you for, or how it may help you realize a dream.

61

It's Not Always About You

At the end of my last message—the one titled, "A Step Already Taken?"—I closed with this suggestion: "If you are feeling divinely inspired to take a certain action, but it doesn't seem to have anything to do with accomplishing a particular goal that you have in mind . . . *do it anyway!*" The context for that statement was the idea that your next divinely guided step may not *appear* to be related to any specific desire that you have, but in a way that you simply cannot see, it is. And if you take that step, it will help you fulfill your desire in a remarkable effortless manner.

Well, here's another good reason to "do it anyway:" *The divine flow is not always about you!* Just as there are people in your life who are there to help *you* move forward, *you* are in *other* people's lives to help *them* move forward. Sometimes you are being divinely guided to say something or do something that will help *someone else* fulfill *his* or *her* dream . . . not necessarily yours. You may be guided to help another person live life more abundantly. Or, you may be guided to help another person live, period. Because this guidance is not about *you*, it may puzzle you at first. One of my readers named Michael shared this wonderful example with me:

Michael was driving down the road one evening when that "still, small voice within" instructed him to stop at the grocery store and buy some bottled water. Although Michael really didn't see the need to buy bottled water at that particular moment, the "voice within" persisted. No matter how much he tried to dismiss it, this intuitive nudge remained very clear and very strong.

So, Michael followed this apparent divine direction and stopped at the store. The second he walked in, he received another clear instruction to go down an aisle to the left. Again, he tried to dismiss this idea because he knew that water wasn't located on that particular aisle. But the "voice" was so compelling, he honored it once more and walked over to that section of the store.

There, Michael ran into a friend of his that he hadn't seen in quite some time. He told his friend that he had felt intuitively guided to stop at the store and go down that particular aisle, but he didn't understand why. At that point, Michael's friend became visibly emotional. The friend explained that he had just received some very disturbing news, and eventually confessed that he was on the verge of doing something that, for him, would be extremely self-destructive.

As the two talked, Michael realized why he had been divinely directed to come to this store . . . and it wasn't just to get some water. It was so he could help his friend deal with his anguish in a more productive manner, which is exactly what Michael did. He offered to spend the evening with his friend, and the healing that took place during their time together that night was nothing short of miraculous.

So, dear reader, do you want to live your life in the divine flow? Then remember to treat everyone in your path as a *potential angel* who is there to help you move forward. But more than that, remember that *you* are an angel *yourself!* Always remain open to divine guidance—even when that guidance doesn't seem to have a whole lot to do with *your* life. *Just do it . . . anyway!*

62

The Pleasures of Life

One of the first big hits by Sting—the world-famous singer and songwriter—was centered around this lyric: "We are spirits in the material world." In May of 2009, I got to see a great example of that. I was in Dallas, Texas, for the first birthday of my grandson, Cole. If you want to actually *see* Spirit, just look into the eyes of a young child. The divine light that comes shining through those eyes is unmistakable. And what fun it is to watch that Spirit enjoying the material world it finds itself in.

My birthday gift to Cole was a small Native American drum from Sedona. Cole immediately began to bang on that drum with relish. You could feel his excitement grow with each and every beat. And the expression on his face seemed to say, "Listen to the sound I can make! Listen! Listen!"

Cole's unabashed enthusiasm reminded me of the time I watched a little four-year-old girl dancing to some music being played by a street musician in Albuquerque, New Mexico. What was particularly interesting about this child was the way she "observed herself" as she danced. She would look at her arms as she waved them in the air. She would look at her feet as she shuffled them across the ground. And she would look at her waist as she swiveled her hips around and around. I felt like I was witnessing that little girl's divine Spirit being fully aware of its presence in this physical world, and consciously enjoying the pleasures that this world has to offer. "Look, I have a body!" "Look, I can move it all around!"

So, you may ask, what does all this have to do with living life in the divine flow? Simply this: Always remember that your enjoyment of life has very little to do with reaching the chosen destinations that you are "rowing" toward. Sure, fulfilling a desire or realizing a dream feels great! But that is just the icing on the cake. The real, deep-down enjoyment of life comes from allowing yourself to appreciate the *entire* journey, and all the wonderful things the journey presents to you along the way.

As you pursue your goals in life, be sure to pause for a moment to appreciate the simple beauty of a tiny flower, and the majesty of a mighty tree. Notice the refreshing feel of a cool, spring breeze . . . the pure, clean scent of approaching rain . . . and the sound of a bird as it sings its splendid song.

Remember that living life in the divine flow is not just about getting where you want to go. It's also about *how you live* as you row. Don't forget to take the time to laugh, sing, play, and read . . . to eat your favorite foods . . . to dance to your favorite music . . . and, if you are so inclined, to bang on a drum. Make sure that you allow your Spirit to do what it really came here to do in the first place—just to enjoy the experience of being alive and in the world!

63

The Game of Life

Have you heard the story about the professional gambler who dies and finds himself in a very peculiar afterlife? He discovers that—at least for him—the afterlife consists of an eternal game of poker that he will be playing with several other deceased gamblers.

He is elated by this prospect, and is delighted when he easily wins the first hand. He is even more excited when he wins the second hand. And when he wins the third hand, he is absolutely ecstatic. However, when he also wins the fourth hand, he is more surprised than happy. And when he wins the fifth hand, he is downright puzzled. Finally, after winning the sixth hand, seventh hand, and eighth hand, the gambler exclaims: "Hey, this isn't any fun! I don't think I'm going to like it here in Heaven." To which, one of the other gamblers replies: "What made you think this was Heaven?"

I decided to share this story, because it makes a good follow-up to my last message titled, "The Pleasures of Life." In that message I wrote about all the delights that life has to offer you, if you will pause long enough—and be present long enough—to notice them and appreciate them.

But life is not always one pleasure after another, is it? As we row our boats down the stream toward the fulfillment of our dreams, we also encounter rocks and reeds, sandbars and whirlpools, unexpected turns and dead-end tributaries— often as a direct result of our own freewill choices. Can you appreciate *those* experiences, as well? Can you appreciate life's *challenges* as well as life's *pleasures?*

The wonderful thing about life is that it is the turbulent parts of the stream that enable you to appreciate the more peaceful parts. You cannot fully appreciate experiences like comfort, freedom, and ease, unless you also know their opposites. The true joy of living comes from learning how to appreciate life *as a whole*—including any rapids or waterfalls you might encounter along the way.

Like the gambler realized in the afterlife, you can't enjoy winning unless you also experience losing. Here's to enjoying the game of life, and remembering that it is the bad hands, as well as the good hands, that keep the game interesting . . . and ultimately, fulfilling.

64

Missing The Boat

Throughout my first book, and even more explicitly in my workshops, I describe about a dozen different ways that we interfere with the divine flow in our lives, and thus delay the manifestation of our heart's desires. Among those ways are these three:

- We consider assumptions to be facts, and we make choices based on that.

- We think we know best, and we remain rigidly attached to our plans.

- We look too far ahead, and we miss the next right step that is directly in front of us.

You might think that after spending more than 20 years learning how to recognize and cooperate with the divine flow, I would be able to easily avoid those three forms of interference. But the fact is, most of the ways that we interfere with the flow are quite subtle, and even an "expert" like me can inadvertently miss or dismiss divine guidance. Here's a good example:

One of the favorite things that Carol and I like to do is to go digging for crystals. Some of the world's best open-pit crystal mines are near Hot Springs, Arkansas. So when we lived in Dallas, Texas—which is only five hours away from Hot Springs—we would go crystal digging regularly.

When Carol and I decided to move to Sedona, Arizona, we figured it would be a very long time before we had an easy opportunity to go crystal digging again, so we planned one last trip to Hot Springs. This time, however, we decided to break from our usual routine. First, we decided that we would try digging at a brand new mine. And second, we decided that we would return home via the scenic route, instead of the Interstate.

Well, the new mine was not what we hoped it would be. We found very few crystals, and those that we did find were small and of poor quality. Plus, the weather was cold and misty, so the digging conditions were pretty uncomfortable. Disappointed, we returned to the nearby cabin we were staying in for the night.

When we woke up the next morning, the sun was shining brightly, and my very first thought was, "Now *this* is a perfect day to go crystal digging!" Carol must have had the same feeling, because she asked me if it was possible to go back to our favorite mine and spend part of the day digging there, before we had to return home. That's when I failed to follow the flow.

I told Carol that it was, indeed, too far to go back, and if we did, we would have to return home via the Interstate, and we would miss whatever beauty the scenic route had to offer us. But get this: I told Carol that without even looking at a map! From what I thought I "knew" about where our cabin was located, I just *assumed* that our favorite mine was too far away, and I never questioned that "fact."

So we stuck to the plan. We left our cabin, and took the scenic route home, which turned out to be nice, but not nearly the spectacular drive we thought it would be.

Only when we got back to Dallas did I take the time to closely look at a map. And guess what I found out? Our favorite mine was virtually around the corner from where we were staying! We could easily have spent one more day digging! Of course, there is no guarantee that we would have found better crystals. And yes, we would not have been able to take the scenic route home. But we quickly realized that we would have *gladly* traded off the scenic drive for the *possibility* of coming back home with some great crystal keepsakes.

Instead, I completely ignored the intuitive thoughts and feelings that both Carol and I were having when we woke up in the morning, and I didn't take the next right step that was being called for in that moment. And what *was* that next right step? To simply look at a map. That's all—just keep an open mind and look at a map! Instead, I made a choice based on an assumption, and I never really questioned our plan.

Dear reader, if an "expert" like me can miss a divine opportunity so easily, what does that mean for people who are not nearly as focused on the flow as I am? How many miracles are we missing in life? How much do we struggle needlessly? How often do we—as the saying goes—"miss the boat?"

I believe that we live in a Universe that is *far* more beneficent that we realize, simply because we are constantly missing or dismissing the divine guidance that we are continually receiving. May we all resolve—right here and right now—to pay much better attention to the flow, and to let go of what we think we "know." Because that is exactly what it takes if we truly want our lives to be more joyful, more fulfilling, and—on top of that—remarkably effortless.

65

Life's Divine Cairns

In the summer of 2009, I started offering Divine Flow Retreats here in Sedona. The very first activity I conduct in my retreats is a guided meditation on a Red Rock formation called Bell Rock. Many people believe that Bell Rock has amazing healing and energizing properties, and it is one of the most popular places here.

If you have spent any time in Sedona yourself, you probably know that it is not extraordinarily difficult to reach the higher parts of Bell Rock. However, without knowing the best way to ascend, you can easily run into a dozen dead ends, and repeatedly encounter crevices that cannot be crossed. To make it easier for hikers to reach the higher vistas, the National Forest Service has placed piles of rocks called "cairns" to guide the way. When you travel from cairn to cairn, you are able to climb up Bell Rock in the most efficient and unobstructed way possible.

And so it is with the divine flow in your life. When you follow your intuition, when you are open to the intuitive guidance of others, and when you pay attention to the divine signs that are all around you, you will find yourself being directed toward the fulfillment of your heart's desires in a virtually effortless and obstruction-free manner.

That doesn't mean that your path will always be direct—a straight line from where you are to where you want to be. Nor does it mean that your journey will be swift. It is common to experience lots of twists and turns along the way, and reaching your chosen destination can take longer than you expected. But if you remain patient, and take one divinely guided step at a time—focusing only on the step that is right in front of you—your journey will still feel like a flow . . . a flow that is helping you get to your highest good in the most beneficial way possible.

Here's to following life's divine "cairns." Here's to noticing and heeding the divine markers that have been placed along the way to help us accomplish our goals without undue struggle or strain . . . and to help us reach even the loftiest of our dreams with ease.

66

Watch Your Step!

The last activity I lead in my Divine Flow Retreats is an optional hike to the top of Mescal Mountain, one of Sedona's lesser-known Red Rock formations. When I first explored this particular area of Sedona, I was painfully reminded of one of the principles for living life in the divine flow: Always keep your focus on your *current* step!

You see, the trail to Mescal Mountain is not only covered with lots of loose rocks, but it also has lots of cacti growing all along the way. If you don't watch where you are stepping, you might slip on the rocks and fall. Or, you might walk right into a prickly cactus—which is exactly what I did. Ouch! Instead of paying attention to where I was walking, I was looking too far ahead, and I suffered the consequence.

The same thing can happen as we pursue our heart's desires. As I frequently mention, living life in the divine flow requires present moment awareness. The divine flow is always showing you the next right step to take to reach your goal. And that step is usually right in front of you, relatively easy to do, and free of painful obstacles. But to *see* that step, you must stay focused in the *here and now*, instead of being focused somewhere in the *future*.

That doesn't mean that there isn't any value in looking ahead and seeing where you want to go. In fact, that's a requirement. Choosing a destination is what sets the whole flow in motion in the first place. But after that, you must return your attention to the present moment, so you can see the next step that the flow is guiding you to take.

It's a back-and-forth thing: You visualize your goal, and then return your awareness to the present. You picture your dream, and then come back to the current moment. If you are *continually* daydreaming about where you are headed, you may *miss the very step* that is leading you there. Or worse, you may make a *misstep* and find yourself sitting by the side of the trail pulling barbed bristles out of your leg!

Do you have a goal you've set that you would like to accomplish, or a dream in mind that you would like to realize? Great! Just remember that getting there is a step-by-step process, and your journey will be a lot more peaceful and a lot more pleasant if you stay focused on each step as it comes along. Happy Trails!

67

Ego and The Flow

I n these messages I sometimes mention the word "ego," and I write about the various ways that choices made from the ego can severely limit your ability to be "in the flow" and fulfill your heart's desires effortlessly.

Usually, the ego is associated with an inflated sense of self-importance—often expressed as arrogance or grandiosity. And it is fairly easy to see how decisions based on those expressions of your ego can lead you into troubled waters.

But did you realize that the opposite is also true? A low sense of self-worth—of being less than others, or undeserving—is also an expression of ego. And, just like an inflated sense of self-importance, a low sense of self-worth can also make life more difficult for you than it has to be.

You might wonder how both of those extremes in self-perception can have the same source. Well, the answer lies in the way that many spiritual teachers define "ego," which is simply, "a thought that you are separate."

Any thought that causes you to feel greater than others, or less than others, is a thought that—in your consciousness—

separates you from others. And since we are all part of that One Divine Spirit that we commonly call God, that means that any thought that separates you from *others* will also—in your consciousness—separate you from that One Spirit, and its loving assistance.

And therein lies the problem. When you are in ego, you are disconnected from G.O.D. (the Guidance Of the Divine), and any decision that you make—even one that is made with the best of intentions—is limited by your own incomplete knowledge and imperfect understanding.

As I have mentioned time and time again in these messages, to live life in the divine flow it is important for you to maintain a *conscious connection with divine direction.* And that means that any thoughts of separation must be avoided. Instead of belittling others and inflating yourself— or the other way around—it is important to consistently affirm the Truth about yourself and others.

And what is that Truth? It is the Truth that each and everyone of us is a beloved Child of The Divine; that each and everyone one of us is *equal* at birth and *equal* in worth to every other person on this planet, and thus, *equally* deserving of whatever it is we want to have, do, or be in life.

May we all enhance our ability to live life in the divine flow through thoughts of *oneness* instead of separation. May we recognize the underlying Truth that every single person in this world is not only our brother or sister in Spirit, but is actually a *part* of ourselves—another wave in that ocean of Universal Energy that gave birth to us all, nurtures us all, and sustains us all.

68

A Surprisingly Powerful Affirmation

When it comes to living life in the divine flow, one of the keys I mention frequently is maintaining a positive attitude, because a positive frame of mind helps you stay open and receptive to divine guidance. One popular technique for maintaining a positive mind-set is through the use of affirmations. In the area of prosperity, for instance, you might make an affirmative statement such as, "I am prosperous," or "Prosperity is mine by divine right, and I claim my divine inheritance now!"

I often use affirmations to remind myself of basic truths that I have momentarily lost sight of. A while back I decided that I needed to once again affirm my financial abundance. But this time, instead of a thought arising in my mind such as, "I am prosperous," this statement occurred to me instead: "There is *no reason* why I can't be wildly prosperous!"

I realize that since that statement contains the words "no" and "can't," it doesn't appear to be extremely positive. Nevertheless, I have found it to be very reassuring. Every time I use that affirmation—for prosperity, or health, or whatever—I feel an immediate sense of relief, and I quickly regain a feeling of positive expectation.

Why? Mainly because that statement reminds me that "reasons" mean very little when it comes to living life in the divine flow. "Reasons" are limited and restrictive in their nature, and they are often based on information that is flawed and faulty, or incomplete at best. You will always find plenty of "reasons" why your heart's desires *cannot* be fulfilled . . . including "reasons" like you are not worthy enough to have what you want, that you are not smart enough to do what you want, or that you are not talented enough to be what you want.

When you make the statement, "There is *no reason* why I can't (fill in the blank)," you are denying the power that "reasons" have over you, and you are, instead, affirming the *real truth* of the matter—the truth that the divine flow operates at a level *beyond* reasons, and beyond *reason itself*.

The divine flow operates in the realm of the *miraculous*, orchestrating things on your behalf in a way that is often beyond comprehension or prediction. And more importantly, the divine flow is completely unlimited in its nature, so anything and everything is possible!

Is there something that you want to experience in your life right now—something in particular that you want to have, do, or be? Then attune yourself to the divine flow and follow the divine directions that you receive. In spite of how things may look to *you*, remember that the Mind of the Divine sees *no reason* why you can't reach your destination with effortless ease . . . *no reason whatsoever!*

69

Networking and The Flow

In 2001, when I was laid off from my 30-year career in advertising, one of my friends in the business said to me, "You'd better start networking!" I cringed when I heard that. Why? Well, for a couple of reasons:

First, I wasn't sure I wanted to stay in the advertising business any longer. And second, the whole idea of "networking" had always made me feel very uncomfortable. At the time, networking felt to me like something that only high-pressure salesmen did . . . you know, passing out their business cards right and left—often inappropriately.

However, as I began my new career as a spiritual author, speaker, and teacher, it didn't take me very long to realize that networking—if seen in the proper perspective—is actually an important part of living life in the divine flow.

As I often point out, rarely—if ever—do you get anywhere in life completely on your own. Usually, you need the help of at least one other person to get where you want to go. In fact, quite often, the assistance of several people, or more, is required for you to reach your chosen destination.

When you tell the Universe what it is you want to have, do, or be in life, you attract these people to you. The Universe literally sends them your way to assist you in fulfilling your desire. These are the people who have the leads, contacts, information, and inside scoop that you don't have. And, as part of your divine flow, they have been divinely inspired to share what they know with you . . . or, to direct you to others who might be of assistance to you . . . or, to take direct action themselves on your behalf. When you recognize these people for who they are, or who they might be, and—with an open heart and an open mind—you engage them in conversation, isn't that networking?

I recently witnessed a great example of this when I took a shuttle van from Sedona to the airport in Phoenix. There were only three other people in the van. One was an artist from Rhode Island, who was returning home after visiting his mother in Sedona. One was a young, aspiring writer from Florida, who was returning home after visiting her parents in Sedona. And one was a tour guide from Sedona, who was on his way to see his fiancé in Germany.

Along the way, the artist mentioned that in a few weeks he would be going to Florida to exhibit his paintings at an art show that is held annually in Boca Raton. However, he didn't know much about that particular show, and he was wondering what kind of paintings he should take.

Well, guess what? As it turned out, the aspiring writer lives just a few blocks from where that art show is held. And not only that, every year her roommate works at that very venue! In just a few minutes, the writer connected the artist to her roommate over the phone, and all of the artist's questions were answered right then and right there.

As for the young writer and her aspirations? Well, she mentioned that she had only recently graduated from college, and was looking for work. When the tour guide heard that, he revealed that his fiancé was the senior editor at a popular magazine—a magazine that was currently hiring writers— and he said he would be happy to have his fiancé contact the young lady.

Amazing, huh? Of course, like most anything in life, networking can be misused—especially when the relationship is one-side and you are just trying to "get something" from the other person. But when you enter into any relationship— even the briefest of encounters—seeking ways that the two of you can be of mutually beneficial service to each other, that's networking as it is divinely designed to be done.

Many of my speaking engagements have come about by just that kind of networking. My first home in Sedona was the result of networking. And networking is responsible for much of the prosperity I have enjoyed in my life.

So, dear reader, do you have a dream that you want to realize? Do you have a goal that you want to accomplish? Then, as my advertising friend said to me in 2001, "You'd better start networking!" Or, as I am more inclined to say: Pay attention to the people who come into your life, and treat them with the honor, respect, and gratitude they deserve as your brothers and sisters in Spirit. Who knows, they may be divinely guided "Earth Angels" who have crossed your path for the sole purpose of helping you fulfill your heart's desires.

Here's to all the people who have been part of the divine flow in my life. Thank you all!

70

Divine Encounters

In my message titled, "Networking," I wrote about the people you "attract" into your life, and how those people are often there to help you accomplish a goal or realize a dream. These divinely orchestrated relationships—no matter how brief—are always beneficial to both parties. And usually, the mutual benefits are obvious. But not always.

Sometimes, the Universe brings two people together for a purpose that is far more significant than either person recognizes or realizes. In 2007 I met a man in Quincy, Illinois who shared his story with me, and it is a perfect example of what I am talking about.

This man, Mac, is fascinated with antique farm equipment, and he has an entire barn—a museum really—filled with inventions that have made farming more efficient and less physically demanding. One day, Mac attended a farm equipment exhibition in a town in far eastern Iowa. Out of all the people who were there, Mac felt "compelled" to introduce himself to one man in particular. This man's name was Skip, and Mac learned that Skip lived clear across Iowa in the border town of Omaha, Nebraska—the same town that Mac's daughter, Connie, happened to live in.

After a few minutes, Mac asked Skip if he knew anyone who had a particular antique grain conveyor for sale. Surprisingly, Skip told Mac that his own family had that very piece of equipment sitting unused on a farm in northwestern Iowa, and they would be happy to sell it.

Delighted by this happy coincidence, Mac offered to purchase the conveyor. The two men arranged to meet in Omaha a few weeks later, and drive up to the farm together to pick it up . . . which is just what they did.

After putting the conveyor on a trailer, Mac and Skip began the long, slow drive back to Omaha. During the course of their conversations, Mac revealed that ten years earlier his granddaughter—Connie's child—had lost her life in a car accident when she was just a teenager. Skip asked where the accident had happened, and when Mac told him, Skip grew very quiet.

Mac went on to explain that another teenager—a boy—was driving Mac's granddaughter home that night, and they were hit by a car that ran a red light. The boy survived, but Mac's granddaughter did not. When Skip heard this, he became quieter still.

After several miles of silence, Skip finally asked Mac what his granddaughter's name was. When Mac told him, Skip paused, then quietly replied, "The boy who was driving your granddaughter home that night was my son."

Naturally, Mac was stunned by this amazing coincidence, and he wondered what the significance of this divinely orchestrated encounter was. The answer came quickly enough. Although Mac, Connie, and the rest of their family had made peace with this tragedy long ago, Mac got the definite feeling that it still troubled Skip—that there was some kind of unfinished business that he had never attended to. And when Mac found out that Skip had never met Connie, Mac felt guided to ask Skip if he wanted to visit her when they got back to Omaha. Skip said yes.

What transpired between Connie and Skip—the mother of one child, and the father of the other—is between them. Mac only knows that hugs were exchanged, tears were shed, and some kind of needed closure was reached.

What I find particularly beautiful about Mac's story is this: There are plenty of things in life that we *consciously know* we want—like a new car, a bigger house, or a better job. But there are also plenty of things we *deeply need*, which we may not be fully aware of—like complete recovery from an old emotional wound. How comforting it is to know that the divine flow can bring us together in ways that not only give us what we wish for on a *surface* level, but can also—*at the very same time*—take care of a desire that lies *beneath* . . . such as a desire to be healed, or a desire to be returned to a state of peace. What a blessing that is. Is it not?

71

The Challenge of Change

In the year 2001, the 11th of September became more than just another day of the year. It became a day that will always be remembered for an event that—for many of us—greatly altered the way we live our lives.

I, for one, was laid off from a 30-year career in advertising as a direct result of what took place that fateful morning. American Airlines was one of my advertising agency's principle accounts, and American decided to suspended advertising for an indefinite period following the attack that used their planes. My agency had to cut its budget. People were laid off. And I was among those people.

It was a dramatic change in my life, but just one of many changes over the years. And I'm sure that you have experienced quite a few radical shifts in your life, as well. Some of those changes may have felt like they were *thrust* upon you. Others may have been changes that you, yourself, *consciously chose* to make. No matter what initiates it, a change of any kind can always be a source of tension and anxiety. Even when a change is obviously for the better, you may still resist it—clinging to a familiar past for comfort. Even when the future seems ripe with positive possibilities, you may still feel uneasy about stepping into the unknown.

If you are going through a major change in your life right now, take a moment to reaffirm what you know to be the Truth. It is the Truth that—with the help of The Divine—everything can be a stepping-stone to a higher good. It is the Truth that you are continually being guided by The Divine to a life of greater happiness and satisfaction, and your job is to remain open and receptive to that guidance by accepting what is, and by maintaining—to the best of your ability—a positive outlook.

Remember that the only constant in life is change. So instead of continually *resisting* change, why not choose to actively *embrace* it? Instead of fighting the current, choose to "row with the flow" and experience the peace that comes from *consciously cooperating* with life . . . even when life takes a sudden and dramatic turn.

72

If It Feels Right, Do It!

In *Time Magazine's* issue for the week of January 11th, 2010, there was an article about Magnus Carlsen, the youngest player in the history of professional chess to achieve No. 1 status. According to Gary Kasparov, a former chess champion:

> "Carlsen's mastery is rooted in a deep, intuitive sense. He has a natural feel for where to place the pieces, and a knack for sensing the potential energy in each move, even if its ultimate effect is too far away for anyone—even a computer—to calculate."

The article went on to state that many of Carlsen's moves are not even considered to be viable options by the experts *until* they see those moves and realize how perfect they are. About this, Carlsen simply says:

> "It's hard to explain, but sometimes a move just feels right."

Dear reader, when it comes to living life in the divine flow, I cannot emphasis enough the importance of paying keen attention to how a potential move in your life *feels*. You make countless decisions every day—some big, some small. And naturally you want all of your decisions to be good decisions—decisions that are divinely guided and divinely supported. But often it is impractical to wait for a divine sign to appear, or for a synchronistic event to occur, to help you make the best choice.

Your own *intuitive sense*, however, is always right there and ready to assist you. Although there are many ways that your intuition can speak to you, most commonly it is through a simple "feeling of rightness." One potential choice just *feels* a little better than the other one.

Although I make a point of nurturing my intuitive sense, and I have always relied upon it heavily for making important decisions, I only recently noticed how much I use my intuition for *every* decision that I make. Not too long ago, someone asked me which restaurant we should go to for lunch. For a brief moment I considered Restaurant A versus Restaurant B, and then I said, "I think we should go to Restaurant A." Later, I noticed that I had used the word, "think." But the fact is, "thinking" had almost *nothing* to do with my choice. I simply imagined myself in Restaurant A, then in Restaurant B, and Restaurant A *felt a little better*. It just . . . well . . . *felt right*. I realized in that moment how almost *all* of the decisions I make in life are *automatically*—and to some degree *unconsciously*—based on how those decisions *feel*.

When Carol and I needed to move from one home to another here in Sedona, I came up with what I thought was a logical plan for moving—what we should do first, then second, then third, and so on. But in the end, we ended up doing things in a completely different order. Why? *Because it just felt right.* And I can honestly say, our move was an extraordinarily smooth one.

Even the message that you are reading right now was greatly influenced by how I *felt* as I wrote it. I make it a practice to read my messages over and over and over again, until every paragraph, every sentence, and every word not only makes sense, but also *feels right.*

Is there a move—either big or small—that you are contemplating making in your life right now? Then go ahead and use your logic and reason to weigh the pros and cons of making that move . . . or of not making it . . . or of making an entirely different move. Just make sure that you pay *special attention* to how each potential choice *feels.*

And if it's time to make a decision and you are *still uncertain* about which way to go? Then make the best choice you can and don't fret about it. Remember—more so in life than in chess—even a *misguided* move can be transformed by The Divine into just another stepping-stone to your highest good.

73

T.R.U.S.T.I.N.G.

A s a person whose livelihood depends primarily on the written word, I always appreciate clever wordplays and creative phrases, including what some people call "backronyms." A backronym is the *reverse* of an acronym. It is an appropriate phrase formed from the letters of a word that *already exists*. For example:

EGO = Edging God Out
FEAR = False Evidence Appearing Real
HOPE = Holding Onto Positive Expectations

A while back, the minister at a Unity church that Carol and I attend mentioned this backronym during his talk:

TRUST = Totally Relying Upon Spirit's Timing

In these messages I often mention the part that *divine timing* plays in the manifestation of your desires, and how that requires a fair amount of patience on your part. If you try to force something into being before the Universe has gotten all the "ducks in row," you may complicate things and delay that manifestation even further. Or, you may create something that is a poor imitation of what the Universe was originally lining up for you. Or, you may fulfill your desire before you are the kind of person you need to be in order to maintain that manifestation for any length of time. However, living life in the divine flow—and fulfilling your heart's desires effortlessly—is not just about *timing*.

It's also about *inspiration* . . . about being open and receptive to divine ideas—the kind of thoughts and insights that fill you with great enthusiasm, and give you a clue as to what you were born on this planet to do.

It's about *nurturing* . . . knowing that the Universe is always supporting you in your emotional development and spiritual growth, by giving you the opportunity to benefit from every single thing that you experience in life.

And it's about *guidance* . . . remembering that the Universe is continually directing you toward your highest good in a myriad of ways, and it is up to you to constantly be on the lookout for that guidance—whether it comes from your own intuition, the intuitive wisdom of others, or the divine signs and synchronicities that are all around you.

Put all of these things together, dear reader, and you wind up with this expanded backronym:

TRUSTING = Totally Relying Upon Spirit's
Timing, Inspiration, Nurturing, and Guidance

T.R.U.S.T.I.N.G. It's a way of being that I constantly try to practice. And I invite you to join me in practicing this way of being, too . . . not just sometimes and in some situations, but—as the first letter in this backronym suggests—*all* the time and in *all* situations. That is, *Totally!*

74

Relying On Wisdom

A while back I received an email from Christy in Peoria, Illinois, who came up with something that makes a perfect follow-up to my message titled, "T.R.U.S.T.I.N.G." It is a "backronym" (reverse acronym) for a word that I frequently use. That word is "row." And Christy's backronym is:

ROW = Relying On Wisdom

Anyone familiar with my work knows that I consider "rowing" to be a very important aspect of living life in the divine flow. Rowing represents the *action step* in the manifestation process . . . but not just *any* action. As I use the term, rowing refers to taking *divinely inspired* action— the only kind of action that will lead you to your chosen destination with effortless ease.

When you "row" you are basing your action on divine counsel, or—as Christy put it—*relying on wisdom*. That means that you must take some time to get quiet, go within, and access the intuitive guidance of your own Divine Spirit.

And you must take some time to thoughtfully consider the insightful guidance that flows forth from the Divine Spirit of others, as well.

To *rely on wisdom*—to R.O.W.—requires you to pause after each and every "stroke of your oars" to attune yourself to the flow, and make sure that you are still going in the same direction that the current is flowing. Said another way, you must pause after each and every step you take to make sure that your *next* step is another *divinely directed* step, instead of a step that is driven by your fear-based ego. It's the kind of step that gives you a feeling of peace and ease, instead of making you feel tense and anxious. And it's the kind of step that is usually confirmed by the appearance of divine signs and synchronicities.

Do you have a certain desire that you would like to fulfill effortlessly? Do you have particular goal that you would like to accomplish with divine ease and grace? Then remember to R.O.W. (Rely On Wisdom), instead of acting out of F.E.A.R. (False Evidence Appearing Real), and making choices based on E.G.O. (Edging God Out).

In short, remember to put your trust in G.O.D. (the Guidance Of the Divine)!

75

When a Door Closes

Has this ever happened to you? You have a particular goal in mind. You begin to pursue that goal, and you feel divinely supported in reaching it, because doors are miraculously opening for you everywhere. You experience an unbelievable stream of coincidences and synchronicities that make your progress incredibly effortless. As you take one divinely guided step after another, you feel like you are definitely "in the flow!"

And then, surprisingly, you run into a closed door. You are certain that the divine flow led you to that door, so you knock on it. But there is no answer. You decide to knock on it again. Still, there is no answer. Frustrated, you knock one more time—a little harder—and the door finally opens. But then the person who opened the door shuts it in your face. You are confused. You are positive that the divine flow meant for you to go through that door. What happened? And what are you supposed to do now?

In response to the first question—What happened?—there is, of course, no single, definitive answer. Maybe you were mistaken about that particular door being part of your divinely prepared path. Or, for some reason, perhaps your goal is no longer in your best interest. Or, consider this possibility: Perhaps the doorkeeper was simply not cooperating with his or her divine instructions to open the door for you, and keep it open.

Remember that, for the most part, the divine flow works through people doing what they are being divinely directed to do. Each of us is continually being guided to take actions that will not only help us fulfill our *own* dreams, but will also help other people fulfill *their* dreams. Unfortunately, people don't always play the part they are being divinely encouraged to play. Sometimes they are simply not in touch with that still, small voice that is inspiring them to take a certain action that will assist or support another person. Other times they *do* sense what they are being divinely asked to do, but their ego gets in the way. They become insecure, resistant, or even threatened in some way. So they hesitate. Or worse, they flat out refuse to take the action that—in their hearts—they know is right. Instead of being part of the divine flow for someone, they close the door in that person's face.

And when *you* are the one facing that closed door—a door that you fully expected to be open for you—what are you supposed to do then? The temptation is to bang on the door again, or try the backdoor, or climb in through a window. Those are the kind of thoughts that might enter your mind. But is that what you are being divinely directed to do? How do you know when an action that you are considering taking is an act of *force* arising from the ego, instead of your *next right step*—your *divinely guided step*?

I wish there was a simple answer for that—a hard and fast rule, or an unmistakable sign. All I can tell you is what I, personally, experience in moments like that . . . which is this: There comes a point when I notice that an action that I am considering taking is accompanied by a sense of tension and anxiety, rather than a sense of peace and ease. There are possible downsides to this course of action, and I can easily see what they are. And the fact that I am even *questioning* this action, instead of feeling sure about it, is a sign to me that I may be moving into the willful world of manipulation and control, rather than "rowing with the flow."

That's when I surrender any and all notions about how my desire is going to be fulfilled. Through prayer and meditation, I seek the guidance of my Spirit, and I become willing to follow that inner guidance—whether it is telling me to move in a whole new direction, or telling me to patiently stay put.

I once had a door that was closed to me for over a year. Then, one day, I *suddenly* felt inspired to knock on that door again. And this time, it swung wide open. I don't know if it was a matter of divine timing, or if the doorkeeper had a change of heart, or if there was a brand new doorkeeper. Any of those things is possible. But none of that matters. Don't forget that your job is never to "figure out" what's going on. It is only to remain open and receptive to your next right step, knowing that *when one door closes, the Universe always opens another.* I hope you take as much comfort in that thought as I do.

76

Hold On To Your Dream

In my last message—the one titled, "When A Door Closes"—I wrote about dealing with the kind of obstacle that suddenly and inexplicably appears in your path, even though you feel like you have been totally "in the flow" up to that point. But what if you *continue* to run into one obstacle after another? What if you are *consistently* inhibited in reaching a particular goal in life, because you are *constantly* encountering uncooperative and resistant people—people whose assistance you need?

What then? Does that mean that you should give up on your dream, because—obviously—it just isn't being divinely supported? Before I answer that question, here are a few things I recommend that you *do* give up on:

Give up on any pre-conceived notions you might have about *how* your dream is going to be fulfilled. Remember that the Mind of the Divine can see a lot more ways for you to accomplish your goal than you can. If you stay too narrowly focused on how it is *you think* you are going to fulfill your desire, you may be limiting yourself, and restricting the manifestation of your good.

Give up on *when* you think your goal will be accomplished. The obstacles that are delaying you from reaching your chosen destination may be serving a very good purpose. Perhaps you are not yet the person you need to be to successfully handle the fulfillment of your desire. Or perhaps circumstances in your life, the lives of others, or the world in general have changed to such an extent, it would not be beneficial for you to fulfill your dream at this particular point in time.

Finally, give up on *what* you think the realization of your dream has to *specifically* look like. Remember that the divine flow is rarely guiding you to *exactly* what you "think" you want. Instead, it is guiding you to what will fulfill you the most, which is usually an *experience of life* that your inner Spirit wishes to have—such as an experience of love, healing, or creative self-expression. And that experience can be manifested in a *myriad* of ways, *not just the one you've specifically thought of.*

Do I dream of being a New York Times Best Selling Author? Of course I do. I think that would be wonderful. But I avoid becoming overly attached to that one specific dream. Why? Because I really don't know—with absolute 100% certainty—that being a best selling author is the "soul-satisfying experience" that I assume it would be for me.

What I *do* Know (with a capital "K") is this: When I share my spiritual journey and understanding with others, I experience a profound sense of joy and satisfaction. And writing a popular book is not the *only* way for me to share my truths and have that experience. I can also do it as a public speaker, as a class leader, as a private instructor, as a minister, or even as an Internet blogger. My job, I believe, is to stay in touch with my underlying desire to share my spiritual insights, and to allow the divine flow to orchestrate the best outcome for that desire—the one that would *truly* be best for me according to my own personal makeup.

So, I pose the question again. In the face of ongoing obstacles, should you give up on your dream? My answer is no. As long as you feel enthusiastic about a particular dream of yours, by all means, *hold on to that dream* . . . but hold on mainly to its *essence*—to the experience of life that dream elicits. Whether your dream is a certain kind of career, or a particular kind of relationship, hold on to how that dream makes you *feel*. Hold on to the tremendous *joy* it brings you. Hold on to the deep sense of *accomplishment* it offers you. Hold on to the extraordinary feeling of *love* it gives you. But let go of the specifics.

By holding on to the essence of your dream, and letting go of the particulars, you allow the divine flow to guide you to something that will be *truly* fulfilling for you—something that will not only be in *your* best interest, but in the best interests of *everyone* . . . and something that may even be *better* than anything you have ever imagined.

Here's to having dreams and pursuing dreams. But most of all, here's to *allowing* those dreams to come true in *whatever way* is the most beneficial way for you.

77

Minor Miracles and The Flow

As I wrote in the Introduction to this book, I define the divine flow as an underlying current that is continually guiding you toward the effortless fulfillment of your heart's desires. If you are new to my work, you might assume from the phrase, "your heart's desires," that I am talking about desires that are extremely important to you, or desires that are exceptionally grand and glorious. And you would be right about that. But you would only be partially right. Because the desires of your heart can also be desires that appear to be relatively insignificant—desires that seem to be fairly minor in the overall scheme of things.

What you once again have to remember is that your "heart" is your "Spirit," and your Spirit has desires both big *and* small—*all* of which, when fulfilled, serve to help you live a life that is more joyful and rewarding. And the divine flow works just as diligently to guide you to the effortless fulfillment of those seemingly *small* desires, as it does to help you fulfill the ones that seem *large* by comparison. Here's an example:

Here in Sedona, Carol and I subscribe to the local newspaper, the *Red Rock News*. Although we always read the headlines on the front page, after that we rarely do much more than check out the entertainment section, or look through the classifieds for an interesting estate sale. One day, though, I felt an unusual urge to grab a cold drink, go out on the patio, and sit down to read the *entire* paper—something I had never felt inclined to do before.

Well, I didn't have to read very far to discover why I had been mysteriously compelled to open the paper. Because there on Page 2 was an obituary for a dear friend of ours—a woman that Carol and I had not seen in quite some time. Her name was Nanette, and for many years she was the head innkeeper at our favorite Bed & Breakfast Inn, The Briar Patch. Before we moved to Sedona, Carol and I stayed at The Briar Patch so often, we formed a lasting friendship with Nanette. She was, in fact, one of the very first guests we invited to our home when we became Sedona residents.

Had I not followed my intuitive guidance to read the paper that day, I would have missed the obituary, and Carol and I would probably have missed the opportunity to attend Nanette's memorial service. As it turned out, though, Carol and I were able to attend the service, and pay fitting tribute to a woman who meant quite a lot to us.

So, was that an example of being divinely guided toward the accomplishment of a major goal in life, or toward the realization of a lifelong dream? Of course not. *But it was the fulfillment of a heart's desire, nonetheless.* In fact, Carol and I would have been *heartbroken* if we had missed the opportunity to join Nanette's other friends and family in a celebration of her life.

I invite you, dear reader, to join me in taking the time to recognize, appreciate, and celebrate *all* the miracles that occur in life—the *major* ones, as well as the *minor* ones. Each and every one of them makes a difference.

78

Forgiveness and The Flow
Part I

I often write about the power of love, and how just a little bit of loving kindness dramatically enhances your ability to live life in the divine flow and fulfill your heart's desires effortlessly. But love has many aspects. And one of the most important of those aspects is forgiveness.

Just as it is with loving kindness, practicing forgiveness becomes its own reward—healing you, freeing you, and restoring your sense of well-being. But it also has a very practical side benefit—that of improving your ability to move easily down the stream in the direction of your dreams.

The reason why is simple, really. As I frequently mention, living life in the divine flow is about being open and receptive to the guidance you are continually receiving from that creative, intelligent, all-pervading energy that we call God—an energy that you are intimately connected to, whether you are consciously aware of it or not.

When you are *unforgiving*—that is, when you are blaming or resenting someone in your life—you are judging that person. And that creates a problem. Because the part of you that judges is your ego. And your ego is the part of you that is *never* open to divine direction.

Your ego is the part of you that literally "Edges God Out" . . . hence, E.G.O. When you are in ego, your mind is closed. And thus, you are no longer receptive to the helpful insights, inspiration, and instructions that come from the Divine Spirit within you. Instead, you must make choices based on information that comes solely from the material world around you—information that is always extremely limited and highly biased.

If you want to live life in the divine flow you must constantly practice forgiveness. Instead of blaming, seek understanding. Instead of shaming, have compassion. Take the time to look beyond a person's outward behavior to see the innocent Spirit that lives at the core of his or her being. Do that, and you will not only be opening yourself up to G.O.D.—the Guidance Of the Divine—but you may also be opening yourself up to the very person who has been sent by The Divine to help you reach your dream.

79

Forgiveness and The Flow
Part 2

In Part 1 of my series on Forgiveness, I said that forgiveness enhances your ability to be open and receptive to divine guidance—to the kind of guidance that can help you fulfill your heart's desires with effortless ease. But consider this: Even if a forgiving attitude did *not* increase your ability to be divinely guided, you would still be well advised to maintain that kind of compassionate mind-set. Why? Because forgiveness directly affects your ability to enjoy life and be happy!

I will never forget the moment when I first came to understand the relationship between forgiveness and happiness. Many years ago there was someone in my life whom I deeply resented. One evening, I was sitting in my car feeling absolutely miserable because of the offense I perceived that this man had committed against me. All of a sudden, I recognized that—on a certain level—I actually believed that I was *punishing* that person by bearing a grudge against him. And yet, the truth was, he probably had no idea how much I resented him. And if he did know, he probably didn't care!

There I was, sitting in my car feeling angry and upset,

while that man was walking down a street somewhere whistling a happy tune! That's when it dawned on me that I needed to forgive that person for *my* sake—not *his*! There is a great old saying that sums up this idea perfectly:

"Not forgiving someone is like drinking poison
and expecting the other person to die."

That's exactly what I had been doing up to that point—trying to make *someone else suffer* by doing something that was *only hurting me*!

Dear reader, I invite you to get honest with yourself—*really* honest. Are you refusing to forgive someone in your life because part of you believes that you are punishing that person with your resentment? And perhaps more importantly, how is that working for you? Are *you*, in fact, the one who is actually suffering because of that negative emotional tie?

Perhaps it is time for you to stop giving that person power over your emotions. Perhaps it is time for you to forgive that person, and allow yourself to be happy again.

80

Forgiveness and The Flow
Part 3

In Parts 1 and 2 of my series on Forgiveness, I wrote in detail about two specific benefits that you receive by forgiving. But the gifts of forgiveness don't end there. In all, forgiving is *for giving* yourself *five* different gifts.

In this message I want to share all five of those gifts with you . . . beginning with the two I have already explored:

1. Forgiving is *for giving* yourself
the ability to be attuned to divine wisdom.

When you harbor resentments, you are in ego—that judgmental state of mind that not only causes you to feel separate from others, but also causes you to feel separate from any kind of Higher Power. When you forgive, you reconnect with that Higher Power—returning to a state of mind that is once again *open and receptive* to divine insights, inspiration, and intuitive direction.

2. Forgiving is *for giving* yourself
the freedom to be happy again.

As long as you bear a grudge against someone, you will be unhappy—feeling frustrated, bitter, or angry. *You* will be suffering, while the person you resent might not even be *aware* that you resent him or her . . . or care! When you forgive, you stop giving that person power over how you feel. You break that negative emotional tie, and free yourself to be happy again.

3. Forgiving is *for giving* yourself
valuable insights about yourself.

Sometimes the person whom you need to forgive is actually "mirroring" a behavioral trait that you may have, but don't want to consciously admit. If you are willing to "look in that mirror," you may find something within yourself that needs healing. For instance, you may discover a long-neglected emotional wound that has been causing you to behave in unproductive ways. But now that it has been revealed, you have the opportunity to heal that wound through a little self-love . . . as well as the opportunity to see that person who is your "mirror image" in a more compassionate light.

4. Forgiving is *for giving* yourself
the ability to enjoy the peace of the now moment.

Whatever it is that is causing you to feel resentful, happened in the past, right? Perhaps it was only yesterday, but it still happened in the past. By harboring those negative feelings, you are keeping the past alive. Generally, the now moment is pretty peaceful. But you rob yourself of that peace by dwelling on something that is not actually happening in the here and now. If you want to be able to enjoy the peace of the present, let go of the past through forgiveness.

5. Forgiving is *for giving* yourself
the power to create a different future.

The future is formed in the present—through the thoughts and feelings that you are having right this minute. If you have dragged the past into the present through unforgiveness, then it is highly likely that you will create a future that is just like the past. If you want a *different* future, forgive what happened in the past—let go of it—and open yourself up to the infinite possibilities that exist when your mind is free of all prior influences.

There you have it, dear reader: The five gifts of forgiveness. Why not give yourself every one of those gifts today?

81

Forgiveness and The Flow
Part 4

In my first three messages on Forgiveness, I focused mainly on the wonderful benefits that you receive when you forgive. But how, exactly, do you go about forgiving? Is it really enough to just look beyond a person's outward behavior to see the innocent Divine Spirit that resides within him or her? Not always.

Sometimes—especially when you are feeling *extremely* hurt or *exceptionally* angry over a perceived offense—you may be willing to forgive, but willingness alone may not be enough to get you over your emotional hurdle. So what do you do then? To conclude this series on Forgiveness, I offer you a simple technique that I find helpful in such instances:

Whenever I feel extremely judgmental towards someone, I imagine something that might have happened to that person as a child that would explain his or her behavior. Could that child have been abandoned, neglected, or ignored? Could that child have been given adult responsibilities too early in life? Could that child have been physically or emotionally abused?

I then see the person that I need to forgive as *still that child* . . . *still* using the same coping mechanism that may have once served to protect him or her from an intolerable circumstance . . . or *still* behaving in a way in which he or she was *conditioned* to behave.

Whenever I do that, I immediately feel compassion for that individual, and forgiving him or her becomes much, much easier. That doesn't mean that I *condone* that person's behavior. And it doesn't mean that I am going to *tolerate* that behavior any longer, either. I see nothing wrong with holding someone accountable for his or her actions, establishing boundaries to protect myself, and taking steps to shield others from being harmed, as well.

The difference is, I no longer *condemn* that person for his or her perceived shortcomings. Instead, through eyes of forgiveness, I look upon that individual as a wounded soul who wants nothing more than to be healed of that wound through my compassion and understanding.

Try it. You will be surprised by how quickly some situations transform for the better when people sense that you are no longer attacking them with your judgments. And, of course, you will be amazed by how quickly your forgiving attitude puts you right back in the divine flow of life.

82

The Ripple Effect

Once in a while I meet someone who has the mistaken impression that if you truly "master" all of the principles for living life in the divine flow, you will never again run into any obstacles or challenges in life. I wish!

It's true, that when you consistently follow divine direction, the *number* of obstacles and challenges that you encounter in life will diminish dramatically. *However,* no matter how good you are at recognizing and cooperating with divine guidance, you are *still* likely to encounter quite a few obstacles and challenges along the way . . . for two very good reasons:

First, there are certain challenges that—on the level of your Spirit—you actually *want* to experience. Why? Because some challenges offer you an ideal opportunity to grow spiritually or mature emotionally—to heal a long neglected emotional wound, for instance, or to expand a limited way of being that is preventing you from living a more fulfilling and joyful life. (For more about this, read my message titled, "Purposely Choosing Challenges.")

The second reason that some obstacles and challenges are unavoidable—even when you are highly attuned to the feel of the flow—is because of something called "the ripple effect." Keep in mind that we are *all* interrelated and interconnected in ways that we can't even begin to conceive of. So, when even *one* of us does not follow the guidance of The Divine, and, instead, makes a choice out of ego—out of fear or frustration, judgment or jealousy—that decision creates a ripple that can go out and eventually affect the *rest of us.*

On a local level, it's like the scenario of a boss who unjustly criticizes one of his male employees; the misjudged employee then goes home and unfairly belittles his wife; the upset wife then kicks the dog when it gets in her way; the confused dog then bites the delivery man; and on and on it goes.

On a global level, it's like the time in 2001 that a man directed his followers to hijack some American Airlines planes and fly them into the twin towers of the World Trade Center. As I wrote in my message titled, "The Challenge of Change," that action had a ripple effect that directly changed the lives of countless people across the country and around the world—including me.

It's a simple case of cause and effect, like the decisions that led to the dramatic downturn in our economy in 2008. We are still experiencing the effect of that ripple, which many experts believe began with some misguided choices made by people working in the financial sector.

So, does being a "master" at living life in the divine flow mean that you will *never* encounter another obstacle or challenge in your life? Obviously not. What it *does* mean, though, is this: *When* you encounter an obstacle or a challenge, you will always know the best way to *respond* to it, because you will be *intimately connected to the wisdom of your Spirit.* You will intuitively know *what* to do, *when* to do it, and *if* you should do anything at all. And even more importantly—because you will be responding from the part of you that is *divine love itself*—your every response will be a *loving* one.

And guess what? When you respond to a challenge with *love,* you create a *brand new ripple*—a ripple that is so great, it has the power overcome, cancel out, or transform all that has gone before it! In fact, there is no ripple in this world that is more powerful than the one created by a simple act of loving kindness.

Why not start your own positive ripple today, dear reader? It begins the instant you treat a challenging person with compassion, or greet a troublesome situation with understanding. Believe me, you are definitely going to like the effect of that ripple!

83

The Magical Power of Love

At the end of my last message—the one titled, "The Ripple Effect"—I mentioned the ripple effect of love, and how just a little bit of loving kindness can go a long, long way. For example, when you treat people with kindness and compassion, they feel loved and uplifted. Because of that, they are much more likely to treat others in their path with the same caring attitude. And those people, in turn, are likely to pass the love along once again. For all you know, one simple act of loving kindness on your part may end up transforming a life or healing a situation halfway around the world!

As powerful as that ripple effect is, though, it still has its limits. Why? Because what I just described was a power confined by the laws of cause and effect—of action and reaction. In truth, love is much more powerful than that. The *true* power of loves goes way beyond the laws that govern this world. It is a power that exists outside of this physical plane we live in . . . a power that works its magic totally unrestricted by the confines of either time or space. It is *this* power that is responsible for the experiences in our lives that we consider to be truly miraculous.

It is the kind of power that choreographs incredible synchronistic encounters between individuals who have similar desires of the heart, but need each other in order to manifest their dreams. An architect with a critically ill child, for example, may one day feel divinely inspired to design a hospital wing for children with similar health challenges. At the very same instant, thousands of miles away, a wealthy benefactor may become inspired to finance just such a project. Before these two people meet—or even know of each other—they both "decide" to vacation in New York City, where they just "happen" to encounter each other at a coffee shop. And . . . well . . . you can fill in the rest.

That, to me, is the *real* power of love. It is a power that sets the whole flow in motion, initiating a complex series of events that weave together in a way that no one would ever have imagined possible. It is a power that *simultaneously* inspires minds, ignites hearts, and orchestrates harmonious outcomes of incredible beauty.

That is *authentic* power—a power that goes far beyond the ripple effect, but still starts in exactly the same way . . . with one, single, loving intention.

Here's to the power of love . . . rippling . . . tripling . . . and manifesting miracles in an instant.

84

Moving Beyond Reasons

In response to extremely challenging situations, one of the things I commonly hear people say is this: "Everything happens for a reason." Well, I agree . . . in part.

I say "in part," because when people say, "Everything happens for a reason," they are usually referring to a *"divine reason."* They are indicating that everything that happens— including every circumstance that seems unwanted—has been *divinely orchestrated* for our benefit, even though that benefit cannot be readily seen at the moment. But is *every* challenge that we encounter in life actually there by *divine design?* Every single one?

Some challenges, no doubt, *are* divinely directed. For example, when your inner Divine Spirit purposely guides you into a challenging situation so you can heal or grow in some way, that situation is certainly part of the divine flow for you. There are also situations that you may *perceive* to be unwanted challenges, but they transform on their own into something beneficial so quickly, you can easily see how those situations were simply misunderstood "bends in the stream."

But again, I ask, is there a *divine reason* for every single challenge you experience in your life?

What about the consequences you suffer when you continually ignore or overrule divine guidance—when you make misguided choices influenced by your ego, or make unguided choices because you are not paying attention to the divine signs? In that case, there is certainly a reason for what is happening. But is it a *divine reason?* I don't think so.

What about the consequences you suffer when *other people* make misguided choices that ultimately affect your life? What happens is certainly happening for a reason. But again, is that reason of *divine origin?* Not the way I see it.

And what about natural disasters, such as a tornado that ravages one half of a town, but leaves the other half untouched? Or freak accidents, like a light fixture that suddenly falls from the ceiling and injures the one person who happens to be standing underneath it? Personally, I believe that natural disasters are just that—*natural,* and not divinely governed. And freak accidents? Odd, but not orchestrated by God.

Dear reader, in a world where troublesome things often seem to happen randomly, trying to make sense out of it all is completely understandable. And to draw the conclusion that everything happens for a divine reason is also completely understandable. But the point I am building up to is this: Searching for reasons—divine or otherwise—is not always constructive . . . especially if turns into blaming others or shaming yourself for what has occurred.

If you can easily see the reason why something has

happened, and you—or others—can learn a valuable lesson from that, terrific! But it is often difficult—if not impossible—to know with complete certainty why things happen the way they do. "Why?" is rarely the most important question you need to be asking. The most important questions you need to be asking are "How?" and "What?" *How* can I heal, grow, or benefit from this experience? And *what* is my next right step to help bring that good about?

Remember that no matter what has happened or why it has happened, there can always be a divine flow *from that point on*—a flow that directs you and supports you in a return to an overall experience of well-being, or even *enhances* your life in some way. With the help of The Divine, every challenge you experience in life can become an opportunity for you to move closer to your dream . . . a chance for you to grow in compassion and wisdom . . . an occasion for you to heal what needs healing . . . or *all* of those things.

Your job is to be *positive* enough to see the *potential* for good in everything that happens, *present* enough to participate in the unfolding of that good, and *patient* enough to allow that good to manifest in its own right time. May you be up for that task.

85

Transformation

Many people believe that Halloween is a night when the line between the physical world and the world of Spirit is exceptionally thin. With that in mind, I want to share a story with you that is not only *appropriate* for Halloween, it is also *inspiring*.

When Carol and I lived in Dallas, Texas, we spent a fair amount of time visiting and caring for Carol's mother, Ethel M. Marsden. Ethel lived in a nearby nursing home, and after years of declining health, Ethel finally made her transition to the next plane of existence. She was laid to rest in her long-time home of St. Louis, Missouri.

A few months later, as a thank-you gift for my support and assistance during that difficult period, Carol bought me a beautiful painting of a dragonfly. Dragonflies were not particularly significant to either Carol or me. But the painting was created by our favorite artist, and he had used our favorite colors—purple and blue—so naturally, we were attracted to it.

Immediately after purchasing that painting, we discovered that in many circles, the dragonfly is considered to be a symbol of transformation. We also found out that certain Native American tribes believe that dragonflies carry the souls of the departed. We had no idea how significant that information would become!

You see, both Carol and I were present at the time of her mother's transition, and Carol, in particular, was having a very hard time letting go of that final, painful image of her mother's withered and lifeless form. One day, Carol felt divinely guided to visit the gravesite of another loved one buried right there in Dallas . . . far from Ethel's final resting place in St. Louis. As Carol stood at the grave, a fluttering motion caught her eye. It was a dragonfly hovering over a headstone a number of rows away. A few minutes later, that dragonfly had been joined by several more. And later still, dozens had gathered at this single spot in the cemetery.

Carol was just about to leave—and was, in fact, in her car—when she noticed that even more dragonflies had now converged at this one place on the grounds. Carol sensed that something very important was happening, and she felt divinely directed to get out of her car and walk over to those dragonflies. And when she did, guess what name was etched on the headstone over which they were hovering. Ethel M! That's right. Out of hundreds and hundreds of graves in this huge, metropolitan cemetery, Carol had been drawn by a group of dragonflies to the one headstone that bore her mother's name.

Immediately, Carol understood the message. Her mother was no longer sick and withered . . . she was *transformed*! As Spirit, Ethel was now dazzlingly beautiful and flying free! And Carol was now free, too—free of that disturbing, lifeless image that had been haunting her thoughts for so long.

Were those dragonflies actually Carol's mother trying to communicate with her? Was Ethel letting Carol know that—as Spirit—she still existed, and that she was once again happy and whole? That's for you to decide.

What I do know is this: We live in a miraculous universe, and we are intimately connected to everything in it—both the seen and the unseen. When you are open and receptive to divine guidance, and when you *follow* that guidance—no matter what form it comes in—you will always receive what you need . . . including the healing of a troublesome thought, or the lifting of an emotional burden.

Here's to Carol for following her guidance, and for reconfirming for us all that we are, indeed, eternal beings . . . and that life never ends . . . it merely transforms.

86

Who's Charting Your Course?

R ecently I was looking for something to watch on television, and I came across a program about researchers
who were investigating the sinking of the Titanic. They
weren't trying to discover why the Titanic sank so quickly.
There were several factors contributing to that, and they are
now known—including bulkheads that were too short, and
rivets that were too weak. What these investigators were
trying to find out was why this mighty ship broke in half as
it sank.

As it turned out, their investigation proved inconclusive.
What *was* confirmed during this program, however, was
something that has long been suggested: that *before* the
Titanic ran into an iceberg, the captain of the ship made a
decision that proved to be disastrous for both the passengers
and the crew.

Hearing that, I was reminded of something that came
up when I was writing the first chapter of *Row, Row, Row
Your Boat*. To stay with the boating metaphor, I described
the *body* as "the physical vessel itself." But I just couldn't

bring myself to refer to the *mind* as "the captain" of that vessel. I settled for "the brains of the boat," instead. Why? Because for many people the word "captain" evokes an image of a wise decision-maker in a crisp, white suit—a figure entirely worthy of our complete and total trust. But is the mind really that trustworthy?

In the case of the Titanic, it seems that the captain might have been influenced by *someone else* on board during that fateful trip . . . Mr. Bruce Ismay. Ismay was the chairman of the White Star Shipping Line—the Line that had built the Titanic, and touted it as both the *biggest* and the *fastest* vessel on the seas.

When the Titanic received news that icebergs were drifting toward their latitude, there is some evidence suggesting that Ismay may have convinced the captain to *speed up* to avoid the approaching icebergs, rather than slow down or change course altogether. The reason? So the Titanic would arrive in New York in record-setting time, living up to its highly publicized reputation for speed.

Do you see the parallel here? Just like the captain of a ship, your mind *does* have the final responsibility for deciding where you want to go, and how you want to get there. But sometimes your mind can be influenced by the "Bruce Ismay" that resides within your consciousness—that is, by your self-serving ego. Disconnected from the One True Spirit that unites us all, your ego will encourage you to make decisions that may benefit *you* in the short run, but are not in *everyone's* best interest in the long run.

Don't let your ego—which can be just as fearful as it

can be grandiose—chart your course for you! That can be a Titanic mistake . . . literally! Always make sure that your mind remains open enough to receive *divine* direction. It's the kind of direction that comes through intuitive nudges, divine signs and synchronicities, and the intuitive wisdom of others. And it's the kind of direction that you can always trust to be in your best interest, as well as the best interests of *all*.

87

The Ego's Will To Survive

During the 20-plus years that I have been practicing the principles for living life in the divine flow, I have experienced countless major and minor miracles in my life. Day after day, the divine flow has consistently responded to my various needs and desires in remarkably miraculous ways—constantly verifying my belief that we do, indeed, live in an intelligent Universe that is continually offering us its celestial assistance.

So why is it that no matter how much I experience the divine flow in my life, turning to that flow for assistance is not something that I always do *instantly* and *automatically*? Why is it that so many of us—including me—can experience miracle after miracle, year after year, and still *quickly revert* to that old feeling that we are *on our own* when it comes to achieving a dream, or contending with a challenge? Why is it that we don't *continually sense* that we are an inseparable part of a Unifying Whole—a Universal Spirit that is always offering each and every one of us its divine support?

One answer to those questions is found in the teachings

of Eckhart Tolle, who writes about the development of our ego-identities, and how those identities—or "I-dentities," as I like to put it—are essentially based on a very strong sense of a *separate self*. Tolle explains how the ego convinces us that we will *literally cease to exist* if we ever allow ourselves to experience a sense of "spiritual oneness" for any great length of time. So we let the ego vigorously assert itself at every opportunity, tenaciously clinging to that sense of "I" in order to survive. Based on that, it's no surprise then, that our initial reaction to any need or issue that arises in life is often, "*I* have to solve this," or "It's all up to *me* to achieve this."

Here's the good news, though: As time goes by, my experience has been that the hours I spend needlessly feeling that "it's up to me and me alone" to accomplish my goals or solve my problems, grows less and less and less. Year after year, I find it easier and easier to *immediately remember* that I am part of a Universal Whole that is continually guiding me toward my highest good. Day by day, I am able to "let go" more quickly, and I am able to "let God" more readily.

And I am certain, dear reader, that if you continue to practice the principles for living life in the divine flow, then you, too, will experience the same thing. You, too, will find the ego gradually losing its ability to dominate your life. And you, too, will experience a greater and greater sense of divine connectedness, enjoying the peace and ease that result from that ongoing state of spiritual union.

88

The Roundabout Way

These days, when someone new to Sedona asks me how to get to Cathedral Rock or Bell Rock (two of our most popular Red Rock formations), I sometimes jokingly reply, "The best way to get there is in a very *roundabout* manner."

Where's "the joke" in that, you ask? Well, you see, the Arizona Department of Transportation just completed a huge road improvement project here in Sedona. As part of that project, many of the major intersections in and around Sedona were turned into "roundabouts"—traffic circles similar to the ones that are common in Europe.

These circular intersections enable drivers who want to turn left, or who just want to cross the road, to do so without having to wait for a green light, or wait on traffic to clear in both directions. Instead, everyone who enters the intersection simply veers to the right, and then moves around the circle in a counter-clockwise direction until they reach the road they want to be on. When everyone is paying attention, everyone gets where they are going in a seamlessly flowing fashion . . . even though it is a "roundabout way" of doing it.

The point I am getting to is this (and you probably saw this coming): When you live life in the divine flow, the best way to reach your destinations in life—the safest way, and the way with fewer obstacles—is often a "roundabout way." Your desired destination may be to the "left," so to speak, but the flow may guide you temporarily to the "right," preventing you from running into something undesirable, or helping you avoid an obstacle that you are not aware of.

I'll never forget the Sunday when a youth group attended one of my talks, and one young lady proclaimed, "I get it! Our church is only a few hundred feet from the highway, and it is tempting to just want to head straight for it when you see it. But if you did that, your car would wind up nose-down in a drainage ditch! The *best* way to get to our church is to pass it by, take the next exit, cross over the bridge, and then come back down the access road. It's the *long* way, but it's the most *beneficial* way!"

And so it is as you pursue your goals and dreams in life. Your job is just to decide *where* it is you want to go. It is the job of the divine flow to figure out *the best way* to get there—which is always a way that is not only beneficial for *you*, but is beneficial for *all involved*, as well.

Here's to living life in the divine flow, and remembering that the "roundabouts" you frequently encounter in life are there for your highest good, and for the highest good of everyone. May you be present enough to recognize these divine detours when you encounter them. And may you be patient enough and positive enough to happily move in any direction that you are being divinely guided to move in.

89

The Human Experience

As I mention in my message titled, "An Easter Reminder," there is a popular saying that goes like this:

You are not a *human being*
having an occasional *spiritual experience.*

You are a *spiritual being*
having a temporary *human experience.*

The fact that the *True You* is a being of *Spirit*—an individual expression of the One Divine Spirit—comes as a great revelation to many. In fact, some people get so excited by that understanding, they seek to experience their divine spiritual essence as much as possible. These people go to every event they can find that promises them some kind of transcendent spiritual experience—an experience that leaves the body and mind behind, and immerses them in a state of pure beingness; or an experience that offers them some other kind of mystical sensation.

There is nothing wrong with having experiences like that. And there is certainly nothing wrong with getting in touch with the true nature of your being. In fact, to live life in the divine flow it is very important for you to stay in close conscious contact with the Divine Spirit that is your essence. That's why I recommend a daily practice of meditation.

However, it seems to me that spending an *inordinate amount of time* pursuing "spiritual experiences" may be missing the point of life. A life spent that way would be better expressed by a saying like this:

You are not a human being
having an *occasional* spiritual experience.

You are a human being
having *frequent* spiritual experiences!

But that is not how the saying goes. It goes, "You are a *spiritual being* having a temporary *human experience*." That means that you are not in this world to *escape* the human experience through the endless pursuit of spiritual ecstasies. You are in this world to *have* the human experience, but to have that experience from the standpoint of knowing that— at your core—you are a Divine Spirit.

As a Divine Spirit, you are in this world to have the human experience of *creating*—of choosing what you want to have, do, or be in life, and using your divine powers of manifestation to bring that about.

As a Divine Spirit, you are in this world to have the

human experience of *loving*—of expressing *divine* love through all of its *earthly* forms, such as compassion, understanding, acceptance, and forgiveness.

As a Divine Spirit, you are in this world to have the human experience of *the physical body*—to enjoy breathing, laughing, feeling the sun on your skin, and eating a big bowl of ice cream . . . all things that you can't do as pure Spirit!

And, as a Divine Spirit, you are in this world to have the human experience of *the physical earth*—to appreciate the wind, the water, blue skies, purple mountains, and endless fields of flowers.

In short, as a spiritual being, you are here to have the human experience of being alive and in the world, and enjoying everything this earthly plane of existence has to offer—both the sweet and the bittersweet.

Dear reader, by all means, go ahead and seek those peak, transcendent spiritual experiences. Have them. And cherish them. But don't forget to appreciate the beauty and the joy that also arise from the *human* experience. After all, isn't that what you came here for?

90

The Devastation of Separation

A lthough there are rarely definitive answers as to why certain tragedies occur in this world—such as the rash of shooting rampages we have experienced in the last few years—I believe that the underlying cause for many of these events is ultimately the same thing: a feeling of separation instead of oneness.

"Oneness" is about our intimately joined relationship with each other . . . a relationship that arises from the fact that we are all individual expressions of *One Spirit*—that creative, loving, all-pervading Spirit that many of us call God.

There are times when we sense that holy connection more than others, such as when we pray, meditate, spend time in nature, or hold a tiny baby in our arms. And the natural result of that sense of connection is a wonderful feeling of well-being.

But all too often we feel disconnected, instead. We forget that we are one with God, and one with *all* of God's children. We feel separate from others, and separate from everything around us. And that sense of separation—of being all alone and on our own in this world—can generate a fair amount of fear. Sometimes that fear—and the anger that often issues from that fear—can be so magnified by mental illness or negative mental conditioning, we witness the kind of destructive behavior that exploded on the campus of Virginia Tech in 2007; Northern Illinois University in 2008; and at a political gathering in Tucson, Arizona in January of 2011.

Although everything that happens in life is an opportunity for us to discover where our blocks to loving are, it may be quite a while before many of us are willing to feel compassion for the lonely souls who orchestrated those horrific events—events which ended the lives of many, many people . . . and forever changed the lives of many, many more.

For now, let us remember that when we judge others—when we attack them, belittle them, and criticize them—we are not only mentally and emotionally separating ourselves from *them*, we are also mentally and emotionally divorcing ourselves from the *One Spirit* . . . from the *All-That-Is* that is God.

May we remember who we truly are at the core of our being: individual expressions of God, as inseparable from our Source as waves are from the ocean. And may we maintain that conscious connection—and the sense of well-being that comes from that connection—by seeing all of our brothers and sisters as equal members of God's family.

91

Why Pride Precedes a Fall

R egardless of your spiritual background, you are probably familiar with the old saying, "Pride goeth before a fall." Originating from a verse in the Book of Proverbs, it simply means that pride can somehow set you up for failure, and lead you down a destructive path. But why is that?

First of all, let's clarify one thing. The kind of pride we are talking about here is not *authentic* pride. Authentic pride is a healthy sense of your own personal worth and value. You recognize that you have been blessed with a unique combination of talents, gifts, and abilities . . . but you *also* recognize that your accomplishments are the result of a *co-creative endeavor* between you and that Divine Universal Intelligence we commonly call God. It's a "we" thing.

The kind of pride that precedes a "fall" does *not* recognize divine assistance. Instead, it credits all achievements solely to the self. It's an "I" thing, revealed in statements such as "*I* did this," or "*I* did that." This *false* sense of pride comes from the ego—that part of you that tends to Edge God Out (E.G.O.).

When you Edge God Out you are no longer open to divine direction—to the divine guidance that is there to help you accomplish your goals and fulfill your dreams effortlessly. Instead, you have only your *own* intellect to rely on. And thus, your ability to make *truly* wise decisions and take *truly* wise actions becomes extremely limited. Struggle—and sometimes, trouble—often follows as a result.

I can't help but wonder if pride, in part, contributed to the downfall of Ted Williams. Ted is the homeless man who made the national news in early 2011 when a video of him was posted on the Internet. People were surprised to discover that this man, who was begging for money on a street corner, had a remarkable gift—a "golden voice" that was ideal for radio and television broadcasting.

Although the overt cause of Ted's trouble appears to be alcohol and drug addiction, Ted said something in an interview that I believe is quite telling. He said that before his life began to fall apart, "he took everything for granted." He was never grateful for any of the blessings that appeared in his life, and he never thanked a Higher Power for any of the good things that came his way.

I don't know if an attitude of gratitude would have been enough to have saved Ted from his "fall," but I *am* certain about this, dear reader: If you want to live a life that is more joyful, more fulfilling, and remarkably effortless, then don't let the "I" in "PRIDE" be your only guide. Remember that you *also* have the help of something *greater* than yourself— the support of a *Greater* Intelligence and a *Higher* Power. And there is no better way to be open and receptive to the divine direction of that Intelligent Power than to consciously acknowledge its presence in your life, and be continually *grateful* for its loving assistance.

As Meister Eckhart, the brilliant German philosopher and theologian, said:

"If the only prayer you ever say in your entire life is 'Thank You,' that will be enough."

92

Thanks For Everything!

The fourth Thursday in November is when citizens of the United States celebrate Thanksgiving Day. It's a day when we express gratitude for all the things in our lives that we really *do* appreciate, but often forget to be *consciously* thankful for, such as food, family, and friends.

Well, here's a challenge for you: Can you also be thankful for the things in your life that you do *not* appreciate? Can you be thankful for the people in your life that you hold resentments against? Can you be thankful for the circumstances in your life that have brought you discomfort, or even pain?

Yes, you can . . . if you see those challenges as opportunities to discover what your blocks to loving are. Yes, you can . . . if you see those challenges as opportunities to heal wounds you may have forgotten you have. Yes, you can . . . if you see those challenges as opportunities to remember how precious life is, and to renew your appreciation for it.

When you look at the challenges in your life as opportunities to mature emotionally and spiritually, *everything* that occurs in your life can be viewed as a blessing. And blessings are something that you are thankful for, right?

So this Thanksgiving, next Thanksgiving, and every day in between, be thankful not only for the "good" in your life, but also for what you judge to be "not so good."

Be thankful for the *entire* experience of life, *including* the opportunities it gives you to grow in wisdom and compassion.

Be thankful for the *entire* experience of life, *including* the opportunities it gives you to grow in your ability to love others—and to love yourself—unconditionally.

Be thankful for the *entire* experience of life, *including* the opportunities it gives you to remember that life itself is a sacred gift—a gift that is meant to be enjoyed to its fullest, and never taken for granted.

I invite you to join me in giving thanks today and every day . . . for everything.

93

Turning Problems Into Possibilities

Every now and then, dear reader, you will end up in a place that you don't like. You won't understand how the problem that you are facing could possibly be part of the divine flow for you, and you will try to figure out *why* you are experiencing that particular challenge.

Is it because somewhere along the way you made an unguided or misguided choice, and now you are suffering the consequences of that choice? Maybe.

Is it because you are experiencing the ripple effect of ego-driven choices made by someone else? Again, maybe.

Is it because you have unconsciously *chosen* this current challenge so you can grow or mature in some way? Once again, maybe.

Is it possible that you are still "in the flow," and simply misjudging what's happening because current circumstances *seem* to be detrimental to you? One more time, maybe.

Maybe. Maybe. Maybe. Maybe. As I point out in my message titled, "Moving Beyond Reasons," it is natural to wonder why things happen the way they do. But dwelling on that mystery incessantly is not particularly constructive. Why? *Because—in the end—it doesn't make any difference!* As I put it in *Row, Row, Row Your Boat*:

> "Regardless of where you are, regardless of how you got there, and regardless of how bad you perceive your situation to be, it can always be a stepping-stone to your highest good . . . if you are willing to look at it that way."

Why something happens is not nearly as important as *how you respond to it*. And the best way to respond to any undesirable situation is to see the *potential for good* that lies within it. It is that kind of positive attitude that keeps you open and receptive to divine guidance—the kind of guidance you need in order to move beyond your current circumstance.

Admittedly though—depending on the severity of the situation—quickly adopting that kind of positive outlook can be a challenge in itself. That's why I recommend that you take the following four steps to help turn a problem into a possibility for good.

Step #1. Accept what is. That doesn't mean that you have to *like* what's going on. Acceptance is simply about allowing a current circumstance to be *the way it is,* and to stop *resisting* it. If you examine your resistance closely, you will see that it is not about moving *beyond* your present situation. It is just a futile effort to fight against the very *existence* of that situation.

Hey, what is . . . *is!* All the resistance in the world is not going to alter that. Refusing to accept something the way it is will only subject you to needless suffering. And as long as you are trying to rewrite history in your head—vainly trying to arrive at a different outcome with thoughts like "This *can't* be" or "This *shouldn't* be"—you will have little hope of moving to a destination that you *do* like. As long as you are focused on how something *should* be, you will restrict the divine evolution of what *can* be. That is why it is said, "What you resist, persists."

Step #2. Stop blaming others or shaming yourself for what has occurred. You cannot judge or hold a grudge, and, at the same time, be open and receptive to divine guidance. When you are in a judgmental state of mind, you are in ego. And the ego is the part of your mind that is not open to divine ideas and divine inspiration.

To move *forward* you must stop looking *backwards*, trying to determine exactly who caused what. Keep in mind that every single person in this world—including you—is doing the best he or she can, based on his or her limited knowledge, imperfect understanding, behavioral conditioning, and emotional wounds. To see the good that lies within a situation, you must also see the good that lies within each and every person involved in that situation. You must let go of your judgments and release your resentments by looking beyond people's behavior to see the innocence that lies within them—the innocence of their *True Self* . . . the innocence of their Divine Spirit.

Step #3. Adopt an expectation of good. Again, that doesn't mean that you have to *like* your present circumstance. You don't have to try to trick yourself into believing that your current situation is—in its present state—"good." But you *do* have to be *open-minded* about what you are experiencing, and realize that—with the help of the divine flow—your situation can *potentially* be good . . . that it can be a stepping-stone to your highest good, a blessing about to bloom, and a miracle in the making.

Remember that the divine flow can guide you to your good from *wherever you are.* You might think that you are "up the creek without a paddle," but the infinite intelligence of the Universe can see an almost unlimited number of ways for you to get to your highest good from your current position. In fact, the very situation you are in may give rise to a divine opportunity that couldn't have existed in any other environment . . . even if that opportunity is just a chance for you to learn a valuable lesson—a lesson that may serve you well in the future.

Step #4. Seek your next right step. Once you accept what is, stop blaming others or shaming yourself for what has occurred, and adopt an expectation of good, you are now in a position to be *truly open* to divine guidance. Generally, there will be some kind of step that you will be divinely directed to take. You might intuitively sense within yourself exactly what that step is. Or, someone else might be divinely inspired to suggest that step to you. Or, you might realize what that step is via a divine sign or a synchronistic encounter.

Remember, though, to seek only your *next* right step—
that *one single step*—because the divine flow only presents
one step to you at a time. A daily practice of meditation is a
great way to maintain a heightened sense of awareness, so
you will more readily recognize that step when it appears.

And there you have it, dear reader: Four steps to help you turn
a troublesome problem into a positive possibility for good.
Four steps to help you become *genuinely receptive* to divine
direction. Four steps to help you transform an unwanted
situation into a stepping-stone to your highest good . . .
which, as it happens, is always the highest good for *all*.

94

A Fable and The Flow

As I mentioned in my previous message—the one titled, "Turning Problems Into Possibilities"—no matter how bad you perceive a situation to be, it can quickly become a stepping-stone to your highest good . . . *if you are willing to look at it that way.* There is a fable I sometimes tell in my talks and workshops that is a wonderful illustration of this principle. And lately I have realized just how perfect this metaphorical tale really is. Here's the story:

> There was once a rancher who owned a donkey. This donkey was more of a pet than a work animal, and the rancher was sad to watch his beloved donkey grow increasingly feeble and blind as time went by.
>
> One day, the rancher noticed the donkey hobbling across a field toward a bucket of oats. Between the donkey and the oats there was a dried-up well, which was encircled by a short stone wall.

The rancher was horrified when the donkey—being half-blind—stumbled over the wall and fell right into the well! The rancher ran out to the well, and looked down into the hole. But the hole was so deep, the rancher couldn't see the bottom. So he listened carefully for sounds of suffering. But he never heard a thing.

The rancher finally assumed that the donkey must have died instantly in the fall. And although the rancher was very sad about what had happened, he felt like this terrible accident might be a blessing in disguise. The donkey's life had ended quickly, and the donkey no longer had to suffer the ever-increasing aches and pains of aging.

Since retrieving the donkey from the well would be extremely difficult, the rancher decided to make the well the donkey's final resting place. He would fill in the dangerous hole with dirt, and then erect a small monument to his beloved animal on that very spot.

Requiring help with this, the rancher asked his friends to bring over some loads of dirt in their pickup trucks, which they did. And then, after conducting a short, but touching memorial service, the rancher and his buddies began to shovel dirt into the hole.

Well, guess what? Although the well no longer produced water, there was still about six feet of mud in the bottom of the hole. And the mud had protected the donkey from harm. Other than being disoriented, and having his legs stuck in the mud, the donkey was perfectly fine—alive and well!

But then dirt starts falling on the donkey's head! And on his back! And all around him! Finally, the dirt had piled up past the donkey's knees. And that's when the donkey's instinct took over.

First with one leg, and then with the others, the donkey slowly pulled himself out of the mud, and stepped up onto the dry dirt. As more dirt accumulated, the donkey stepped up again. And then again. And then again. Imagine how shocked the rancher was when the donkey suddenly appeared at the top of the well! What a delightful surprise that was!

You get the point, right? Quite literally, the dirt that was supposed to *bury* the donkey became his "stepping-stone to a higher good!" And the lesson for us should be equally obvious:

We, too, blindly fall into holes. And when we think we've hit bottom, sometimes the world adds insult to injury and throws dirt down on us. The difference between people and the donkey, though, is this: We often let the dirt pile up to our necks—or even over our heads—before we are open to seeing the next right step that is right in front of us!

Unlike the donkey, we spend all our time blaming the people who dug the hole, or shaming ourselves for stupidly falling into it. We rant and we rave about the injustice of it all, and in that judgmental state, we fail to notice that the very elements that make up our circumstance can provide us with a way out of our predicament.

But now I see that there is even more depth to this story than I originally thought. For when the donkey got to the top of the well, he was no closer to the oats than he was when he first fell into the hole. And if you have "fallen into a hole," dear reader, the same may be true for you.

Although it is possible for the divine flow to instantly open a portal that leads directly from the bottom of the hole to a goal that you are trying to reach, more often than not, the next right step that you will be divinely guided to take will simply be a step that is designed to help lift you up and/or *rectify* the situation that you are in.

There may be a step that helps you heal emotionally or mature spiritually, or a step that helps you restore something that was damaged or lost . . . but those steps won't necessarily move you any closer to your original destination. There are consequences to going through life blindly—that is, making choices based on fear and ego, rather than continually seeking divine guidance. And when you fall into a hole, there may be quite a few steps that have to be taken, and quite a bit of time that might have to pass, *before* you feel like you are once again heading toward your dream.

Whether it's a step that heals something, reveals something, or repairs something, it's a great comfort to know that the divine flow is continually providing you with what you need to learn and grow, so you can once again glide toward your goal with effortless ease. Remember, though, it's up to you to *recognize* that step when it appears. And it's up to you to *take that step* . . . and the one after that . . . and the one after that.

95

When The Flow Appeases You

As I mention in my message titled, "Don't Believe Everything You Think," one of the key principles for living life in the divine flow is letting go of what you think you know . . . and that includes letting go of any specific destination—any specific goal, dream, or desire—that you believe is best for you.

Any destination that you have in mind is, at best, just an *approximation* of what your *heart* desires—of what your *inner Spirit* really wants to experience. And the fulfillment of that *underlying desire* is what the flow is continually trying to guide you to. If you remain rigidly attached to a goal that is *different* from what your heart wants, your journey is likely to be a difficult one, because the Universe is simply not supporting you in reaching that particular destination.

That doesn't mean that it is completely impossible for you to reach a destination that is not divinely supported. You certainly can. If you row against the flow long enough and hard enough—literally *forcing* your way forward—it is quite possible for you to wind up exactly where you want to be.

But it is also quite possible that you will *regret* where you end up, because the destination you reach will turn out to be unfulfilling, or fraught with problems.

Here's an interesting question, though: What does it mean when you *do* seem to be rowing *with* the flow—when doors miraculously open for you, and opportunities miraculously appear—and yet the destination you reach *still* turns out to be extraordinarily unsatisfying?

A while back I received that very question from Robin, one of my readers in Australia. Robin had fulfilled a dream of 25 years to own and operate a combination café/bookstore located in a small country town 360 miles from her longtime home in Sydney. Accomplishing her goal had been virtually effortless. Doors had divinely opened for Robin, and opportunities had appeared serendipitously. And yet, within one month, Robin knew that this was not what she wanted to be doing for the rest of her life. The work was repetitive and backbreaking. The locals preferred to give their business to other locals instead of an "out-of-towner." And Robin greatly missed her daughter, her friends, and the culture of the big city. Robin has since sold her business and moved back to Sydney.

So, paraphrasing Robin, I ask the question again: What does it mean when the Universe seems to be completely supporting your journey, and yet the destination you reach isn't satisfying, or it creates a whole new set of problems for you?

One answer to this puzzling scenario is that you are, in fact, exactly where you need to be, because the challenges you are facing are something that—deep down inside—you *do* want to experience, so you can grow spiritually or mature emotionally. The answer I want to focus on in this message, however, is a slightly different one. It is the simple fact that sometimes the flow will *help* you get where you want to go, so you will *finally let go* of your fixation on that particular goal, and once again become willing to consider a *different* destination—a destination that is *truly* best for you.

You might think you know yourself pretty well, but there is always the possibility that you aren't perfectly suited for the goal that you are pursuing. There is always the possibility that there is a destination out there that might be a much better match for your unique talents, abilities, and preferences—a destination that, in the end, would be much more rewarding for you.

Like I said at the beginning of this message, to row with the flow you have to be willing to let go of what you think is best for you. If you remain overly obsessed by one particular goal, the divine flow might eventually *appease* you. That is, the divine flow will *help* you get where you want to go, so you will find out—through firsthand experience—that you don't really want what you think you do.

Sometimes, the best way to find out what truly makes you happy is to find out what *doesn't* make you happy. And sometimes, that is exactly what the flow is doing. It is helping you become clearer about yourself—about what you *truly do like*, what you *truly don't like*, and what you *genuinely need* out of life. And what a blessing that increased clarity can be.

Dear reader, as you row your boat down the stream toward the fulfillment of your dreams, please remember this: Whether you are experiencing turbulent waters and unexpected obstacles, or you are enjoying a journey of ease and grace, your job always remains the same. Your job is to spend a little time each day in prayer, meditation, and/or contemplation, *seeking only your next right step,* and then being willing to *take that step* . . . even if it becomes apparent that you are being divinely guided to a destination that is different from the one you originally thought was best for you.

96

The Power of Divine Dreams

As I list in my message titled, "Identifying Intuition," there are many ways that your inner Spirit can speak to you. And one of those ways is through your dreams.

Although it is common for me to experience the guidance of my Spirit through a thought that suddenly pops into my head, or through a subtle—but telling—feeling or physical sensation, divine dreams are rare for me. And by "divine dreams," I mean dreams that are so clear, so meaningful, and so helpful, there is little doubt that they are "heaven-sent."

What follows are three dreams that helped Carol and me deal with some troubling issues in a manner that was remarkably direct and effective:

DREAM #1

I had this dream about 20 years ago, when I working at an advertising agency in Dallas, Texas. There was one man at this agency with whom I was always butting heads. We could never see eye to eye, and we argued about almost everything incessantly.

One night I dreamed that this man and I were at it again—yelling and screaming and stomping our feet. Suddenly, another person entered the room, looked around, and said, "Oh, I'm sorry. I was looking for some adults."

When I woke up the next morning, not only was that dream still clear in my mind, but its meaning was also crystal clear. I was behaving like a little child! My heated exchanges with this man were little more than childish temper tantrums that I was throwing because I couldn't get my way!

After that dream, I am happy to say that I finally began to act my age, and behave like the 40-year-old professional I was. I finally grew up a little!

DREAM #2

This dream also occurred while I was working at the advertising agency I just mentioned. I had been assigned a permanent partner to work with—a lovely lady I'll call Linda. Our partnership was supposed to be ideal, because we were both very much alike—perfectionists.

Can you see the potential problem here? Two perfectionists don't work well together when their ideas about perfection differ! On a personal basis, I really liked Linda, because I could relate to her persnickety ways. But our professional relationship was quickly growing tense and uncomfortable.

Then, one night, I dreamed that Linda walked up to me in the lobby of our office building, and we embraced. And as we embraced, I felt genuine love for Linda. I didn't feel like I was "in love" with her exactly, but I certainly felt a very deep sense of *compassion* for this lady.

And guess what? When I woke up the next morning, that warm, tender feeling stayed with me. And from that point on, I was able to treat Linda with the loving kindness that she deserved. Sure, we still had our differences of opinion. But after that dream, I was able to work things out with her in a much more patient and respectful way. My heart had opened up, and our troubled relationship was healed.

DREAM #3

If you have already read my message titled, "Transformation," you may remember that after Carol's mother passed away, Carol was disturbed by the last image she had of her mother—that of a withered and lifeless body. Although Carol knows that our Spirits live on, she just couldn't get that painful picture out of her mind. But Carol was finally relieved of that emotional burden due to the miraculous appearance of some dragonflies. These dragonflies—which symbolize transformation—appeared at such a unique and meaningful time and place, it was clearly a divine reminder for Carol that her mother was not that lifeless form. Her mother was *transformed*! She was now a beautiful Spirit—lively, loving, and flying free!

But there's more to the story than that. Because shortly after Carol's burden was lifted, she had a dream. In this dream Carol was looking over an audience seated in a large auditorium. Suddenly, Carol heard a voice whisper, "Your mother is here." Excited, Carol quickly responded, "Where?" At that moment, Carol's mother—now looking very happy and very healthy—stood up in the center of the crowd and loudly proclaimed, "I'm right here! And I'm not dead!"

Thanks to that divine dream (and thanks those dragonflies), the image that Carol now holds of her mother is strictly a beautiful one—a vibrant picture of everlasting life and unending love.

Dear reader, have you ever had a dream that helped you recover from something painful? Have you ever had a dream that helped you heal a relationship? Have you ever had a dream that answered a pressing question that you had, told you your next right step, or guided you to something you greatly needed?

Whether your answer is yes or no, I invite you to *nurture* your ability have divine dreams. Before you go to bed each night, take some time to affirm for yourself that you are *open* to receiving a message from your Spirit, and that you will clearly remember that message and completely understand it. It also helps to have a pen and paper nearby, so you can write down your dream the moment you wake up.

Here's to receiving divine assistance from your inner Spirit . . . not only when you are awake, but also when you are asleep! Here's to the healing and revealing power of divine dreams.

97

Disasters and The Flow

When a disaster occurs—like the devastating earthquake and tsunami that recently struck Japan—we often turn our faces to the sky and cry, "Why, God? Why?" In our attempt to make sense out of what has happened, we desperately seek some kind of "divine reason" for it all. And that is completely understandable.

But in this physical world we live in—a world that is not only influenced by the choices of man, but also by the natural forces of wind, water, and shifting ground—things happen . . . tragic things, sometimes. And the simple fact is, there may not be a "divine explanation" for it.

As I stated in my message titled, "Moving Beyond Reasons," a better question to ask is not *why* something has happened, but now that it has happened, *what* is our next right step? What is that divinely guided step that is not only in our own best interests, but is also in the best interests of all?

Once again, I want to remind you that no matter what has happened or why it has happened, there can always be a divine flow *from that point on* . . . a *healing* flow that directs us and supports us in our return to health, wholeness, and an overall experience of well-being. The challenge, as always, is remaining open and receptive enough to hear that still, small voice that is continually telling us the best way to help ourselves, and to help each other.

At this moment, somewhere in the world, there may be people experiencing a time of tragedy—a time of shock and grief, confusion and sadness. Let us send our love and light to all those people who are in too much pain right now to sense any kind of divine flow in their lives. Or, better yet, let us offer those people our aid in whatever way we feel divinely inspired to . . . and *be* the divine flow in their lives.

98

Feeling Overwhelmed?

Fairly often, people will tell me how overwhelmed they feel by everything that they need to do—and *want* to do—in their lives. Their day-to-day responsibilities, combined with all the things they believe they need to do in order to accomplish their goals and dreams, is just too much. Do you ever feel that way? Do you ever feel overwhelmed by it all? The way I look at it, there are three main reasons why you may, at times, feel overwhelmed ... but *unnecessarily* so.

The first is laboring under the impression that it's up to you—and you *alone*—to accomplish what needs to be accomplished. If that's what you think, then yes indeed, completing your "To Do List" will not only *feel* like a daunting task, it *will be* a daunting task. Never forget that you have *celestial assistance* in life! It's the kind of assistance that comes mainly through *divine guidance*—through steps that are suggested to you by your own intuition, by divine signs and synchronicities, and by others who are divinely inspired to share their wisdom with you. When you remember to consciously look for—and be open to—divine direction, you will find that you can accomplish a multitude of tasks in an incredibly effective and efficient manner.

The second reason why you may feel overwhelmed is because you are simply not in the *now moment*. You are looking way too far ahead, imagining all at once—and thus, *experiencing* all at once—every step you think you will "probably" have to take to fulfill your desires. Do you know with *absolute certainty* that you will really *have* to take *all* of those steps? And even if you do, keep in mind that you generally get where you are going in life by taking *one step at a time*. When you focus *only* on the step that is right in front of you—the step that is right here, right now—it is almost impossible to feel overwhelmed.

Which brings me to the final reason why you may feel overwhelmed. You believe that you have identified your next right step, but you are feeling anxious about taking that step because it is a *really big* step. Hey, if you are feeling overwhelmed by the enormity of a step, then that step is probably *not* your next right step! Why? Because the divine flow never requires you to "bite off more than you can chew."

One of the telltale signs of a next right step is that it is relatively easy to do. The divine flow does not ask you to take giant leaps. Instead, it offers you tiny little baby steps that—when taken one right after another—move you effortlessly down the stream in the direction of your dreams.

Think small! Maybe there is a step that you are completely overlooking because it seems so insignificant, like visiting a certain website to get a little more information about something. Or, perhaps there is a step that you are not noticing because it doesn't even look like a step to you, like accepting that invitation to a friend's party. Who knows what helpful person you might meet there.

If you want to stay in the flow, be sure to pay attention to—and take care of—all of those "little" things that seem to just "pop up" in life. Stay in the present moment and concentrate only on the task at hand. And continually seek—and be receptive to—divine direction in all of its various forms. Do those things, dear reader, and instead of feeling *overwhelmed* by it all, you will feel *overjoyed* by it all!

99

Divine Discernment

If you follow the national news at all, you may be familiar with the case of the self-help author and motivational speaker, who was charged with manslaughter after three people died in a sweat lodge ceremony that he conducted here in Sedona. In addition to the three people who lost their lives, eighteen other people became seriously ill during this tragic incident.

Usually, a sweat lodge ceremony is reasonably safe, because the person in charge of this sacred ritual continually monitors the well-being of the participants, and allows anyone to leave the lodge if they are experiencing severe, physical discomfort. Although the leader of this particular sweat lodge did not *physically* restrain anyone from leaving, one survivor of the ordeal claims that those who did attempt to leave—or complained about their distress—were strongly encouraged to "push through it." In other words, they were encouraged to endure their discomfort, to persevere, and to literally "sweat it out."

Whether you believe this man was guilty of an actual

crime or not, there is little doubt that the kind of mind-set he was exhibiting, combined with his influence as a trusted spiritual leader, had—in this instance—a disastrous result. And what does any of this have to do with living life in the divine flow? It points to the importance of practicing discernment whenever someone encourages you to "push through" a problem.

Although the accomplishment of a goal or the realization of a dream may require a great deal of patience on your part, the divine flow will never ask you to "push through" anything—that is, "force" your way forward. Nor, usually, will it require you to endure extreme conditions of any kind. Generally speaking, the path of the flow is always one of grace and ease. Instead of being directed to force your way *through* an obstacle, you will be guided to go *around* that obstacle, or—through the power of divine love—that obstacle might *dissolve* right before your very eyes.

That's not to say that being in the divine flow *always* feels completely comfortable. There may be times when the divine flow will purposely invite you to step out of your personal comfort zone. But if you look closely at what your personal comfort zone is, you will see that is usually a "box" that was *artificially* created by your own personal history and conditioning . . . and it feels good to finally move beyond that limited—and limiting—space.

It appears, though, that the leader of this sweat lodge was doing far more than asking people to move beyond their personal comfort zone. He was inviting them to tolerate extreme discomfort, and encouraging them to ignore what their bodies were trying to tell them. There are physical limits to what the body can endure, and to what the body can do. And even though professional athletes are continually stretching those boundaries, those expansions happen very gradually, and in very tiny increments.

Dear reader, there are going to be plenty of times in life when you will run into a formidable obstacle that seems to be blocking you from reaching your desired destination. And there will probably be well-meaning people around you who will encourage you to "push through it." But please remember, no matter what anyone encourages you to do, and no matter how much you respect his or her advice or opinions, it is up to *you* to decide what is best for you.

Never forget that your most *valuable, reliable,* and *consistent* source of guidance is always *your own intuition.* Even if someone makes a suggestion that sounds like it is "in the flow" and not at all forceful, it is still up to *you* to access you inner sense of "knowing" to decide whether that advice is right for you or not.

Regardless of what people say, or what the signs and synchronicities *seem* to indicate, it is always important to practice *divine discernment*—to get quiet, go within, and get in touch with that subtle, inner sense that helps you distinguish between "yes, this feels right for me," or "no, this doesn't feel like it is in my best interest." As Rev. Suzanne Bishop of Payson, Arizona wrote to me: "I have learned the importance of taking personal responsibility for my own well-being—to not allow anyone to override my internal guidance, and to resist the efforts of someone else to push me beyond what I intuit is good or safe for me at the time."

I hope you understand that I am not asking you to always ignore the suggestions of others. In fact—in addition to divine signs and synchronicities—one of the primary ways that you receive divine guidance in life is through other people. For the most part, though, that information should just be used to *confirm* what your own *heart* is telling you. In the end, every decision that you make, and every action that you take, should be based on the wisdom that lies within—on the wisdom of your very own inner Spirit.

100

The Secret for
a Merry Christmas

December 25th is the day that many people celebrate the birth into this world of the being called Jesus. There are many different opinions about the exact nature of this extraordinary man's mission on this planet. But I do believe there is one aspect to his life that most people can agree upon: Jesus was the perfect example of living a life of unconditional love. And he made it quite clear that we would all benefit greatly by living our lives in the same loving way.

Fortunately, loving others is one of the most natural things in the world for you to do. For I believe that love is not only *in* your nature, it *is* your nature. As an individual expression of Universal Divine Love, love is the essence of who you truly are at the core of your being. And you know what? It feels good to express the truth of who you are! It feels good to love!

Many people believe that *being loved* is what feels good, but that's only how it appears. The fact is, when someone extends love to you, you don't automatically feel good. What you feel is *safe enough* to love that person back. And loving that person back is what feels good. It is *being love*—not *being loved*—that is the real source of your happiness.

Conversely, when you perceive that someone has attacked you in some way, it's not what that person has done that makes you feel bad. What feels bad is judging that person for what has occurred, and no longer extending love to him or her. It is *not* being yourself—*not* being the love that you are—that is the real source of your unhappiness.

When you experience all the good feelings that come from loving, you experience one of life's greatest truths: the truth that love is its own reward. When you love, you feel happy. When you love, you feel joyful. When you love, you feel downright . . . well . . . merry!

So, do you want to have a truly *merry* Christmas this year, and *every* year? Then be true to yourself! *Be* the love that you are this season, and a merry Christmas will be yours, indeed.

IOI

You Deserve Something More

I have noticed a subtle form of self-sabotage that I would like to bring to your attention. It concerns any goal or dream you may have that is particularly ambitious—a desire of your heart that is exceptionally great, grand, and glorious.

That kind of desire is like a destination that lies further down the stream than other destinations that are closer, simpler, and easier to reach. Because of the "distance" that is involved, a great deal of patience may be required on your part as you "row with the flow" toward the fulfillment of your dream.

As months go by—or even years—maintaining your dream can be a challenge. As more and more time passes, you may be tempted to scale back your dream. Without even realizing it, you may gradually move into a mind-set where you expect to manifest something *less* than what you originally desired.

It's true that in my book and in my workshops, I do talk about allowing the flow to guide you somewhere that is *different* from what you planned on or expected. But *different* does not mean *mediocre*. Different means that the manifestation of your dream may not resemble your original intention, but it will be *equally fulfilling*. It will be a destination that brings you so much joy and satisfaction, it will feel every bit as great, grand, and glorious as you originally imagined.

Dear reader, do you have a grand and glorious dream in mind? Terrific! Then don't settle for second best. Avoid the temptation that might eventually arise to replace your dream with a less satisfying—but more quickly fulfilled—one. If you begin to look for less, that is all you will see, and you may miss the flow's attempts to guide you to something greater.

Remember, as a beloved Child of The Divine, you are inherently worthy of *whatever* it is—in essence—that you desire. As author Sarah Ban Breathnach put it so well: "You deserve nothing less than something more!"

Made in the USA
Charleston, SC
01 April 2014